THE A-Z OF [illegible]OUS SHROPSHIRE

STRANGE STORIES OF MYSTERIES, CRIMES AND ECCENTRICS

JOHN SHIPLEY

The History Press

For Harry and Jack,
two fantastic grandsons

First published 2017

The History Press
The Mill, Brimscombe Port
Stroud, Gloucestershire, GL5 2QG
www.thehistorypress.co.uk

British Library Cataloguing in Publication Data.
A catalogue record for this book is available from the British Library.

ISBN 978 0 7509 7034 1

Typesetting and origination by The History Press
Printed and bound by CPI Group (UK) Ltd

Contents

About the Author

Retired managing director John Shipley lives in Bridgnorth in Shropshire, and is now a full-time writer. A Wolverhampton Wanderers fan, he is the author of a number of Westerns, as well as football books.

Also by John Shipley

Aston Villa Champions 1980/81
Nottingham Forest Champions 1977/78
The Little Book of Shropshire
The Nottingham Forest Miscellany
Wolves against the World: European Nights 1953–1980
Wolverhampton Wanderers Champions 1953/54

Acknowledgements

I would like to take this opportunity to publicly thank and acknowledge all the people, individuals and organisations that have helped with the compilation of material for this book and without whom the project could not have been completed: Adrian Pearce of the Shropshire History website: www.shropshirehistory.com, The Shropshire Library Service, the staff at Bridgnorth Public Library, Andrew Pattison, Chris Piggott of NSW Australia and Gail Stokes of Cheshire for their help with the Pigott family. My thanks also go to the compilers of information of the Local History Societies of Broseley and Dawley; to Shropshire Promotions, and to BBC Shropshire. And to everyone who has encouraged my efforts with snippets of information.

My best thanks go to my long-suffering wife Kate and my son Peter, for their immense contribution – rewrites, additional facts, and proof checking, plus my good friends Eric Smith and Mike Thomas for their input. And finally to my editor Matilda Richards and the staff at The History Press.

I must also pay tribute to the other authors of works about the county, in particular Richard Gough for his history *Antiquities and Memories of the Parish of Myddle*, and Charlotte Sophia Burne (1850-1923) for her books on Shropshire folklore; also to Edith Pargeter (Ellis Peters).

The material for this book has been compiled and assembled from personal research, archive material, various websites and printed matter, and of course word of mouth, all of which has been used in good faith.

Whilst every effort has been made to check and re-check the facts and items in this book, the publisher and author bear no responsibility for the content. Where possible, permission has been sought.

And lastly, please forgive me if I have not included any of your particular favourite curiosities.

Introduction

Like the title says, *The A–Z of Curious Shropshire* is a book for the curious. It draws on the long and unique heritage of the county, and is a compilation of the curious, strange, and mysterious stories that bring to life a glittering galaxy of facts about a much-loved county. You will find superstitions, larger-than-life eccentric characters, anecdotes, historical events, tales of ghostly goings-on, scandals, crimes and murders, together with curious legends and folklore – some more believable than others. There are tales of bewitchment and conflict, of heroes and villains, all laid out in an easy to read A–Z format.

It's said that curiosity killed the cat, but hopefully this old adage will prove to be completely untrue for any cats who read this book. That titan of literary figures, Dr Samuel Johnson, described curiosity as 'one of the permanent and certain characteristics of a vigorous mind', so those of you with a vigorous mind can take a bow.

History has always held a fascination for me, not just the monumental dates and the derring-do of our famous heroes, but the little nuggets of local history and of the people who populate an area, together with the sometimes weird and wonderful customs that intertwine with their lives.

My wife and I relocated to Bridgnorth forty-eight years ago, leaving behind the polluted smoke and smog of the Black Country for the good clean air of Shropshire. We have never regretted that decision. In Shropshire we found a county of many contrasts; a beautiful marcher county littered with historic castles and irresistible scenery.

With so many curious stories abounding about Shropshire, it made my choice of what to include and what to leave out a challenging proposition, so please forgive me for any I have been unable to include.

This book is great for dipping into, but can equally be enjoyed from cover to cover.

I hope you enjoy reading this book as much as I have enjoyed putting it together.

John Shipley, 2017

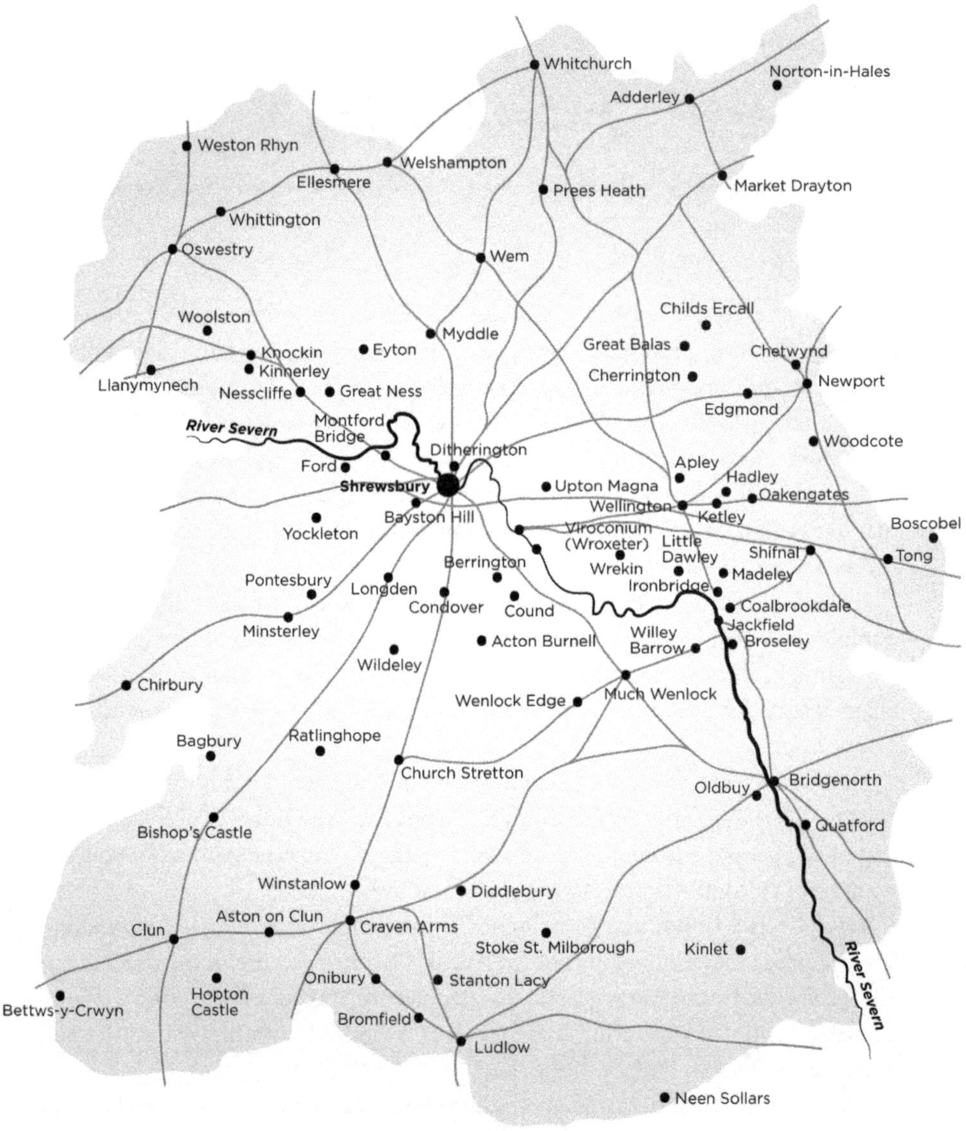
Whitchurch
Norton-in-Hales
Adderley
Weston Rhyn
Welshampton
Ellesmere
Prees Heath
Market Drayton
Whittington
Oswestry
Wem
Woolston
Myddle
Childs Ercall
Knockin
Eyton
Great Balas
Chetwynd
Kinnerley
Cherrington
Newport
Llanymynech
Nesscliffe
Great Ness
Edgmond
River Severn
Montford Bridge
Woodcote
Ditherington
Ford
Apley
Shrewsbury
Upton Magna
Hadley
Oakengates
Wellington
Ketley
Bayston Hill
Yockleton
Viroconium (Wroxeter)
Boscobel
Little Dawley
Shifnal
Tong
Berrington
Wrekin
Pontesbury
Madeley
Longden
Ironbridge
Condover
Cound
Coalbrookdale
Minsterley
Jackfield
Acton Burnell
Willey Barrow
Broseley
Wildeley
Chirbury
Much Wenlock
Wenlock Edge
Bagbury
Ratlinghope
Church Stretton
Bridgenorth
Oldbuy
Bishop's Castle
Quatford
Winstanlow
Diddlebury
Aston on Clun
Clun
Craven Arms
Stoke St. Milborough
Kinlet
Onibury
Stanton Lacy
Hopton Castle
Bettws-y-Crwyn
Bromfield
Ludlow
River Severn
Neen Sollars

SHROPSHIRE

The A–Z of Curious Shropshire

A

ACTON BURNELL

~ The Birth of the English Parliament ~

Around 7 miles south of Shrewsbury lies Acton Burnell, a tiny community of timber-framed, black and white cottages mixed in with buildings of grey-green stone, a place where a monumental event in the history of England took place.

Although the exact date is not certain, at Acton Burnell some time between 1283 and 1285, King Edward I held the first parliament at which commoners were invited to participate – seen by many as the first steps to democracy. The king's most probable reasoning for such a bold step was simply that he needed money to continue his campaign to subdue the Welsh nation, and also to impeach

The wonderfully atmospheric Acton Burnell Castle.

Parliament Barn, Acton Burnell.

and execute Prince David of Gwynedd, the last native Prince of Wales, who had recently been captured.

Edward's chief minister at that time was his friend and advisor Robert Burnell, Bishop of Bath and Wells, and Lord Chancellor of England. Burnell built Acton Burnell Castle, a thirteenth-century fortified manor house, set in the area known as the Marches. Acton Burnell was just one of his many estates: he reputedly owned more than eighty manors, spread over nineteen counties. The only building at Acton Burnell large enough to hold such a huge gathering of invitees – barons, courtiers, advisors and soldiers, in addition to the king's large retinue – was the great barn adjacent to the castle, known today as Parliament Barn. Sadly all that remains of this building are two gable ends, which stand within the grounds of Concord College. The atmospheric ruined shell of Burnell's red-sandstone manor house castle with its embattled towers and decorative crenellations still stands, a picturesque example of a thirteenth-century manor. (Note: some historians prefer to belive that this parliament was actually held at Shrewsbury Abbey.)

One of the laws passed by that parliament became known as the Statute of Acton Burnell, which gave protection to creditors.

The castle is now under the administration of English Heritage.

ADDERLEY

~ The Great Pew Dispute ~

Adderley is a quiet place these days, but there was a time prior to the start of the English Civil War when its church was the scene of a war of attrition.

The two most prominent families in the area were the Royalist Needhams of Shavington Hall and the Puritan Corbets of Adderley Hall, who had been bitter rivals for centuries. Scandalous goings-on that had long festered came to a head in a dispute over seating in St Peter's church. Both families felt they were the rightful lords of the manor, and therefore much higher up in the scale of importance than the other.

In the early 1600s, the Needham family had their own priest and worshipped in their own private chapel at Shavington Hall, independently of the local Adderley parish church of St Peter's. All that changed when this method of worship was banned by order of Queen Elizabeth I, and the Needhams were forced to attend services at the local church.

The first problem for the Needhams was that there was no direct road from Shavington Hall to St Peter's church. Sir Robert Needham's solution was to have his coachman drive the family's carriage to the church in Adderley via a shortcut across their neighbour's land – Adderley Park. That neighbour was Sir John Corbet, and he was not best pleased with the Needhams trespassing on his land without his permission. In actual fact the route to the church and the village of Adderley across Corbet's park had been a right of way for as long as anyone could remember, however, it was little more than a cart track, which the Corbets had never kept in a state of repair and in wet weather became a quagmire, impassable for carriages.

Arriving at the church for their first service under the new regime, the Needhams were horrified to learn that the family, despite Sir Robert Needham being the official lord of the manor, had been allocated seating with the ordinary folk in the nave of the church rather than in a prominent position in the chancel, where they saw their neighbour, Sir John Corbet, and his family seated in their own private family pews in the chancel facing the vicar. At that time Sir John Corbet was a patron of the church, and his ancestors had themselves once been lords of the manor of Adderley.

Sir Robert complained at length at what he saw as a slight against him and his family, stating his belief that he should have been allocated a family pew in the chancel by right, and that in any case he and his family should be given precedence as the most prominent family in the area.

The dispute had the effect of rekindling an earlier feud when the Corbet lord of the manor had the authority to demand, in times of war, forty days' military service of the Needhams in return for his patronage. An agreement had been reached with the Needhams whereby this period of service was commuted to the payment of a sum of money, a contract which had lapsed sometime in the fourteenth century.

Sir John Corbet's reaction to Needham's complaints was to demand monetary payment of the old feudal obligation, which Sir Robert Needham disputed, refusing to pay one penny. Sir John Corbet retaliated by blocking the route across his land, putting up a hedge and having a ditch dug. At the same time he flatly refused to take any action regarding Sir Robert's complaint about the seating in the church.

The local clergyman, Edward Wooley, took it upon himself to try to resolve this portion of the dispute. As rector of the church he too was allocated seating in the chancel, and as he was a bachelor with no family he invited Sir Robert and his family to use his family pew in the chancel, thus granting the two families equal status when inside the church. Unfortunately this arrangement did not last, because the rector met a girl, fell in love and got married, then reclaimed his family pew. Despite a series of bitter arguments, the Needhams found themselves relocated back to a pew in the nave of the church.

The situation was further complicated when in 1625, on the accession of King Charles I, Sir Robert Needham was created Viscount Kilmorey for services to the Crown in Ireland. Although this was an Irish peerage, it meant that the nave was certainly no place for the family of a lofty Viscount. However, this was trumped when Sir John Corbet was honoured with an English baronetcy, with Corbet arguing that an English peerage took precedence over an Irish one.

St Peter's church, Adderley. The previous church on this site was the scene of the Adderley Pew Dispute.

Lord Kilmorey's solution was to petition the Lord Bishop of Coventry and Lichfield for permission to rebuild his private chapel at Shavington Hall, for which he eventually obtained a licence. In 1629, the restored chapel was reconsecrated.

However, Sir John Corbet wasn't done yet, and eight months later instigated a suit in the Court of Arches to have the consecration declared invalid, which was partially successful. The ruling allowed that only limited types of services could be held at the new chapel, such as preaching, prayer and celebrations of the Lord's Supper. Burials, for instance, still had to be carried out at the church.

The death of Viscount Kilmorey in 1631 changed nothing: Sir John Corbet would not let the old man rest in peace. Needham's son, Robert Needham, the second Lord Kilmorey, now instigated proceedings of his own against Sir John, which were heard by a special commission at Market Drayton, who overturned the ruling of the Court of Arches. Needham also took up the cudgel regarding the blocked right of way and, on 14 May 1632, the Court of Wards and Liveries ordered Sir John to reopen the right of way, which he eventually did, but not before a series of acrimonious claims and counterclaims had been made. The route was open, but Sir John flatly refused to do anything to improve or repair the condition of the track.

In 1633, matters descended further when one of Sir John Corbet's servants, a man by the name of Darbee Margh Killaree, died. Sir John, as patron of the church, forced Mr Wooley, the rector of St Peter's, to bury the Irish footman near the place where he sat in the chancel of the church, 4ft above the place where the first Viscount Kilmorey had himself been buried. To add insult to injury, the footman was buried in a shroud, not a coffin.

The second Viscount Kilmorey was away at the time, but upon hearing what Sir John had done was rightly incensed at this slur on his family's honour. He petitioned the Earl Marshal of England, Thomas Howard, Earl of Arundel, to issue a decree on the matter. His pleas were successful and in 1634 Sir John Corbet was ordered to have the body of the footman exhumed and reburied in another place.

In 1634, Corbet was at the heart of Shropshire opposition against forced loans imposed by the king, by criticising the levying of 'Ship Money' (the ship tax – more of this later), another of King Charles I's taxes imposed without the consent of Parliament. Sir John was summoned to appear before the Privy Council of England, accused of making speeches 'to his majesties disservice, and the animating of others to refuse payment of the muster master's fee'. He was incarcerated in Fleet Prison for six months but was never brought to trial.

While Sir John Corbet languished in the Fleet, Viscount Kilmorey secretly petitioned the king to grant permission for him to build a chapel onto the chancel of St Peter's church in which his family could worship. A licence for the work was issued by the Archbishop of Canterbury, William Laud, and work commenced in 1637. The chapel was lavishly decorated with emblems of Needham heraldry.

Lady Corbet now waded in; she obtained a key to the new chapel and took a group of her servants to the church to occupy the new chapel. This early example of a sit-in protest lasted several weeks, until finally they were forcibly ejected. Unhappy at this expulsion, the Corbets returned with an armed guard.

Viscount Kilmorey again protested to the Archbishop of Canterbury, but before any further action could be taken, the outbreak of the English Civil War took precedence. In any case, Corbet was protected by parliamentary privilege, and William Laud had already been impeached and thrown into prison, awaiting execution. And so the Adderley pew dispute was relegated to the back burner.

As fervent Royalists, the Kilmoreys (Needhams) supported King Charles, whereas the puritan Corbets supported the rebel Parliamentarians. At the outbreak of the English Civil War in 1642, Viscount Needham joined the Chester Garrison, and was later at Oxford during the Royalist surrender to Parliamentary forces. He was subsequently fined £3,560 for being a Delinquent Royalist – a sum he negotiated down to £2,360 but which was still a large sum of money in those days. He was again arrested in 1651, when Charles II passed through Shropshire on his way to the Battle of Worcester. Two years later, having lived quietly, Robert Needham, 2nd Viscount Kilmorey, died at Dutton in Cheshire on 12 September 1653.

Sir John Corbet died in June 1662 at the age of 68. He was buried in the chancel of the parish church in Market Drayton, St Mary's.

The north transept of St Peter's church, Adderley.

APLEY

~ *Superstition* ~

In the nineteenth century a woman by the name of Molly Tart lived in a cottage in the tiny settlement of Hadley, a few miles outside Wellington. Molly worked for many years in the gardens of Apley Castle, the stately home of the Charlton family (long since demolished). Molly was famous locally for being superstitious to the point of madness. For instance, if the first person she saw when she opened her door to go to work in the morning was a woman, she would bang the door shut and stay in her cottage for the rest of the day. On the days when she saw a man first she would happily set off for work, but, if the first person she chanced to meet along the way was a woman, she would spin on her heels and hot-foot it back home for the day.

The rent on her cottage was due every quarter day (the four dates in the year when rents were due, servants were hired, and school terms started), and she would set off to arrive at eight in the morning to pay her rent, but when she knocked on the door if it was opened by a female then all thoughts of payment were forgotten, and Molly would turn away and go back home.

Her boss at the castle understood her superstition and always tried to ensure that it was either him or one of his sons who opened the door to her. There is no record of how long she kept her job!

ASTON ON CLUN

~ *The Arbor Tree* ~

Just a short way past the Kangaroo Inn, on a bend in the road towards Clun, passers-by are rewarded by the sight of the wonderful Arbor Tree of Aston on Clun, a huge native black poplar bedecked with the flags of many nations, sited in a delightful tiny picnic area. The flags are hung from long poles fixed to the boughs of the tree.

A tree has stood on this spot for hundreds of years, although the present tree is not the original. This one was grown from a cutting of the old tree, which sadly blew down during a storm in 1995.

The story behind the 'dressing of flags' has a number of supposed origins: some say it dates back to prehistoric times when it was the custom to celebrate the coming of spring, when trees burst into life with new foliage after the cold of winter, blessed as a symbol of new life.

Another belief is that the decoration has its origins in fertility rights, practised by shepherds in Clun forest in Celtic times. The shepherds worshipped Bridget, or Brigid, the goddess of fertility, and whose shrine was a tree on which tribal

The flag-bedecked Arbor Tree at Aston on Clun.

emblems and prayer flags were hung. The blessing of the goddess was sought by brides. Bridget/Brigid eventually became St Bridget/St Brigid or St Bride. Celebrations took place at St Bride's tree.

After the restoration of the monarchy on 29 May 1660, King Charles II proclaimed 29 May as Oak Apple Day, a holiday when trees would be dressed with flags and other such things. The tree was the centre of festivities, later becoming known as Arbor Day at Aston on Clun.

It was on 29 May in 1786 that local landowner Squire John Marston brought his new bride, Mary Carter, to the village, where the Arbor Tree had been dressed with flags. The young bride was so enamoured with this ancient custom that she wanted to preserve it. Her efforts were successful for the custom continued until 1954, when the tree was entrusted to the care of Hopesay Parish Council, who happily continue the tradition to the present day.

According to the nearby information board, Aston on Clun is the only village in Britain where Arbor Day is still celebrated.

Every year on the last Sunday in May, the tree is decked with flags which are left flying for the rest of the year. The wedding of John Marston and Mary Carter is commemorated by a pageant of local children in period costume of the 1700s, and after the ceremony a huge fête is held on Arbor Field with children's rides, tug-of-war, and fun for all the family

ATCHAM

~ *The Ghost of Mad Jack Mytton* ~

Lining one side of the old A5 main road around 4 miles to the south-east of Shrewsbury are a group of tiny thatched cottages, designed by John Nash, that form the bulk of the settlement of Atcham. Near the two bridges across the River Severn, on the eastern bank and opposite the elegant gateway to Attingham Park, lies the red-brick Georgian inn, the Mytton and Mermaid. The building is a splendidly atmospheric, Grade II listed hotel, built in 1735.

The Grade II listed Mytton and Mermaid Hotel at Atcham.

This popular hostelry, previously called the Talbot Arms, is reputedly haunted by the ghost of John (Mad Jack) Mytton of Halston Hall, a Regency rake and true English eccentric, whose vast inheritance disappeared like water running through his fingers. This madcap daredevil regularly risked his life doing crazy things. He reputedly drank up to six bottles of port every day. He also kept 2,000 dogs, plus more than sixty finely costumed cats, in addition to a bear called Nell.

One day, dressed in full hunting attire, Jack rode the bear around the hall until the animal balked at being pricked by a spur, and bit Jack on the leg. The bear also attacked a servant, and was thus put down. Jack also allowed his favourite horse, Baronet, the run of the house.

In 1834, at the age of just 38, Jack died in King's Bench debtor's prison in Southwark, having squandered all his money.

Legend has it that on the way to Halston chapel, Jack's funeral procession stopped off at the Mytton and Mermaid, in those days a well-known coaching inn, to partake of some refreshment, and now the ghost of this true English eccentric is said to haunt the hotel once a year on his birthday – 30 September.

B

BAGBURY

~ The Bagbury Bull ~

In Hyssington parish, on the border between England and Wales, there is a bridge known as Bagbury Bridge, which spans a brook that forms the border between Shropshire and old Montgomeryshire. Nearby at Bagbury Farm, in times gone by there lived an evil squire, noted for his cruelty. When this horrible man died his spirit remained restless and returned, not in the form of a man, but as a roaring, raging bull, who haunted the farm buildings after 9 p.m., roaring so loud as to shake the timbers of the buildings and the slates from the roof. The nuisance could not be tolerated, and so the villagers approached a local witch, asking her to put a curse on the squire, which she agreed to do but only for a price. However, her spells did nothing to change the wicked spirit's behaviour, which was making everyone's life a misery; his restless spirit would not sleep, and his ghost was proving to be far worse than the living version.

Now the villagers appealed to the local clergy for help, and in the age-old tradition, twelve priests assembled to lay the ghost. With lighted candles the clergymen, one of them blind, prayed and chanted until they managed to entice the bovine spirit into Hyssington church, but once inside the bull went mad, charging around so much that it cracked the wall of the church. However, the priests refused to give up and finally prevailed in laying the ghost, and sealing it in a snuffbox. It was at that point that the evil spirit spoke to them, maliciously imploring the priests to lay him under Bagbury Bridge, so that every female who passed over the bridge would lose her child, be she human or animal. According to one version of the legend, the priests refused such a request and sent the snuffbox to the Red Sea, where they believed the ghost would be laid for 1,000 years. Even so, for years afterwards folks crossing the bridge would tread very lightly so as not to risk waking the spirit of the Bagbury Bull.

A second version of the story is that the snuffbox was buried under Wernddu Lane Bridge over the River Camlad in Churchstoke. A third says that the box was left under a flat stone in the marsh at Pennerley. And a fourth version tells us that the snuffbox rests inside a tightly laced boot which has been laid beneath the doorstep of St Etheldreda's church in Hyssington. Which story do you believe?

BAYSTON HILL

~ Air Ace ~

This is the story of a Second World War hero, Shropshire-born air ace Eric Lock (19 April 1919–3 August 1941). Eric Stanley Lock was born in Bayston Hill near Shrewsbury, attending school at Prestfeld. It was whilst still at school that he experienced his first flight at the cost of 5 shillings, with Sir Alan Cobham's Air Circus.

Eric started work in his father's quarrying and farming business, joining the Royal Air Force Volunteer Reserve, the RAF version of the Territorial Army, when rumours of impending war with Germany started. When war came, Eric was called up, and was trained to fly Spitfires. Commissioned Pilot Officer, at the end of May 1940 he was posted to Number 41 Fighter Squadron based at Catterick, Yorkshire, returning to Shropshire briefly to marry Peggy Myers, a former Miss Shrewsbury.

Patrols from Catterick proved to be boring for the young pilot as the German Luftwaffe concentrated their efforts on attacking targets in the south of England, however, on 15 August 1940 Eric shot down a twin-engine Messerschmitt 110 bomber. Following this, Lock and his squadron were posted to RAF Hornchurch in Essex. Two days after arriving, on 5 September, Lock brought down two Luftwaffe bombers over the Thames Estuary, before a bullet from a Messerschmitt ME 109 fighter wounded him in the leg. Despite this, Eric still managed to shoot the German down. Next day, Lock shot down a Junkers 88 bomber, and three days later bagged two more Messerschmitt 109s, then on 11 September he shot down another Junkers 88, plus a Messerschmitt 110. His tally was now eight German aircraft in one week, bringing his total kills to nine. His gallantry was rewarded with his first Distinguished Flying Cross (DFC). The citation told how the young pilot 'displayed great vigour and determination in pressing home his attacks'.

His next kill was an enemy aeroplane that he chased all the way across the English Channel, finally shooting it down over Boulogne. A mere three weeks after receiving his first DFC he was rewarded with a second DFC; he had shot down fifteen German aircraft in only nineteen days. This citation praised his 'great courage in the face of heavy odds, and his skill and coolness in combat'.

Lock's squadron was ordered out of the front line for a well-earned rest, returning to action in October 1940. Another ME 109 shot down brought his total to twenty, but in his next dogfight with ME 109s he came off worse. On 8 November his Spitfire was badly damaged, resulting in him having to make a forced landing; luckily he escaped injury.

On 17 November Lock's squadron attacked a large formation of seventy ME 109s. Lock shot down one and set fire to another before his cockpit was raked by German bullets and cannon-shells, inflicting wounds to Lock's right arm and both legs. One of the bullets knocked the Spitfire's throttle lever wide open, at the same time knocking the lever off, resulting in the Spitfire leaping forward out of the dogfight at top speed – more than 400mph. Alone at 20,000ft, and only able to use his left arm, Lock had no way of slowing down the racing engine. Somehow he managed to manipulate the plane down to around 2,000ft, before cutting his engine and searching for a suitable place for a crash-landing. The plane glided to earth in a field 2 miles from an RAF base, but even so, he had to wait in the cockpit for two hours, bleeding and in pain, before he was eventually found by two soldiers who carried him to safety on a stretcher improvised from a greatcoat and rifles.

Eric Lock woke up in hospital to learn he had been awarded the Distinguished Service Order (DSO). The citation paid tribute to his 'magnificent fighting spirit and personal example'.

Three months and fifteen operations to remove pieces of shrapnel from his legs followed, Lock remaining in hospital until May 1941, except for a trip to Buckingham Palace to receive his decorations.

Lock reported back for duty in July 1941, and was promoted to Flying Officer, with a second promotion following not long after, this time to Flight Lieutenant, commanding a flight of Spitfires with 611 Squadron.

The Battle of Britain now won, the RAF fighter squadrons concentrated their focus on long-range sweeps over occupied Europe – known as Rhubarbs. In his first few weeks back in battle Lock shot down four German aircraft, bringing his total to twenty-six.

However, on 3 August 1941, returning from a sweep over northern France, Lock spied a group of German soldiers on a road near Calais, and swooped down to the attack – he was never seen again. It is thought that his plane was most likely brought down by ground fire, however, no wreckage of his aircraft was ever found, nor was his body recovered. Shropshire's air ace has no known grave.

Eric Lock's name is proudly inscribed on the Runnymede Memorial in Surrey, together with those of 20,000 brave British and Commonwealth airmen and women who were lost during the Second World War, many without trace.

The total number of fighter pilots who fought Goering's Luftwaffe in the Battle of Britain was 2,354 from Britain and 574 from overseas. Of this total, 554 pilots were killed in the battle, while a further 791, including Eric Lock, were killed subsequently.

Eric Lock is remembered in Shropshire. His birthplace of Bayston Hill has a road named after him, and the bar in the Shropshire Aero Club, Sleap, the old wartime airfield, is named in his honour.

⁂ BERRINGTON ⁂

~ *The Lion and The Knight* ~

In an alcove in the fourteenth-century side aisle of All Saints' church, Berrington, 5 miles south-east of Shrewsbury, is the figure of a cross-legged knight carved from one solid piece of oak, wearing a suit of fourteenth-century armour, helmet, and spurs. The knight's face is scarred, his head on two diagonally placed cushions, his hands steepled in prayer, and at his feet is half a battered lion. The knight's identity has been lost in the mists of time, although it is thought he may possibly have been a member of the Lee family of Langley, near Acton Burnell, who were patrons of All Saints' church. Whoever he was, the locals call him 'Owd Scriven' or 'Old Scriven'.

The legendary story of 'Owd Scriven' of Frodesley tells of a knight who, whilst on his way to meet his lady love at Eaton Mascott 4 miles away, encountered a lion by a stile at Banky Piece, Shropshire. The lion savagely attacked the knight, and the two fought intensely, the fierce animal badly mauling the knight's face. Finally the knight was able to draw his sword and with one mighty blow cleaved the lion in two.

Some may find the story of a lion a little beyond belief, for long after our sceptred isle parted from the European mainland, there weren't many lions to be found in Shropshire. There is a thought that the creature at the heart of this legend may in fact have been a wild boar, which is much more believable. Go take a look at the effigy and make up your own mind.

The effigy of 'Owd Scriven' in All Saints' church, Berrington.

BETTWS-Y-CRWYN

~ *The Pedlar's Stone* ~

Bettws-y-Crwyn, a few miles west of Clun, is a small, remote village set on a windswept hilltop over 400m above sea level. It is one of a number of English villages to have a Welsh language place name – the name roughly translates to Chapel of the Fleeces or Skins. It is so called because it housed the Shepherds' Chapel, as it sits near to the ancient drovers' road from Wales to England across the Kerry Ridgeway. The parish includes the hamlets of Anchor, Quabbs, and Hall of the Forest.

On a hillside not far from the village, on a piece of rough grassland and heather, is a large stone known by two names: the Pedlar's Stone, or the Cantlin Stone. The stone measures about 2ft across and is engraved with the inscription: 'W.C. Decsed, here buried 1691 at Bettws'.

The stone is a memorial for a pedlar, William Cantlin, who died on the hill in January 1691, at the spot where the stone is situated, whilst walking between two farms to sell his wares. There are various thoughts on how he died: that he suffered a heart attack; or that he was overcome with hypothermia; or that he was set upon, robbed and murdered. Bettws parish won the dispute with Kerry parish as to who should bury the poor man, whose body is said to rest in the graveyard of St Mary's church in Bettws.

There is an old tale that says that the parish, not certain of the pedlar's name, didn't want to bury a nameless man, and so named him Cantrell, a combination of Can't and Tell, which over time morphed into Cantlin.

Next to the stone is the Botfield Cross. The original limestone Celtic cross, erected in 1858 by Beriah Botfield, botanist, bibliographer and MP for Ludlow, fractured and fell down in 1974, and was replaced by a new cross, which is now surrounded by a wooden fence.

Between 1980 and 1990, a free music festival was held at the site, which subsequently moved to Llanbister.

BISHOP'S CASTLE

~ *A Scam* ~

Living in Bishop's Castle many years ago was a miserly old devil who buried all his money, 40 sovereigns, convinced that if he left it buried for one whole month, its value would be doubled. He had been told of the certainty of this by some devious person who he had recently become acquainted with.

The miser was rubbing his hands as he dug up the hoard, only to discover that he had of course been duped – what he found was not 80 sovereigns, but 80 brass

The House on Crutches Museum up the Cobbles in Bishop's Castle, connecting High Street to Market Square.

buttons. Strangely, his new friend had disappeared from the community, and the old man was left to ruminate upon his greed, and gullibility.

BOSCOBEL

~ A Bed Fit For A King ~

Following the defeat of his army at the Battle of Worcester on 3 September 1651, Charles Stuart (later King Charles II) escaped northwards, fleeing capture from Cromwell's Roundheads (no doubt remembering what they had done to his father, Charles I). Charles had been crowned King of Scotland at Scone Abbey on 1 January 1651 and, supported by the Scots, was persuaded to invade England in an attempt to regain his crown, crossing the border into England in early August.

The Battle of Worcester turned out to be a bit of a rout for Charles and his supporters. Legend has it that Charles dodged out of the back door of his headquarters in the Cornmarket, near St Martin's Gate, as the Roundhead soldiers entered through the front. Figuring his cause would be lost forever if he was taken, the king escaped through an unguarded gate and fled north in company with Lord Derby, Lord Wilmot, Charles Gifford, and a party of other loyal Royalists. The king and his followers stopped in Ombersley (at was is now the King's Arms) for refreshments. From there they rode the short distance to Hartlebury, where it was decided that it would be more prudent for Charles to part company with most of his followers; so he, Lord Wilmot and Charles Gifford continued on to White Ladies Priory in Shropshire, a property owned by the Gifford family. They passed through Hagley and Pedmore, stopping at Whittington Manor House, where more refreshments were taken (curiously it is now a restaurant), intending to get to South Wales and from there take a ship to France.

Lord Derby and his party were captured at Kidderminster and executed. Parliament put a bounty of £1,000 on Charles' head, together with a notice that whoever gave him assistance would be killed in a horrible manner.

The king's party finally arrived at White Ladies Priory, a large timber-framed house built on the site of a medieval nunnery, early on Thursday 4 September, and was cared for by Gifford's tenants, the sympathetic Penderel family, who disguised Charles as a woodsman, cutting his hair in the process. Charles Stuart was 6ft 2in tall and no shoes could be found to fit the large royal feet, so it was necessary to slit the largest shoes that could be found in order to make them fit better.

Richard Penderel led Charles to Spring Coppice near Coven Heath, and they hid there, evading a company of Roundheads who had earlier ransacked another of Gifford's proporties, Boscobel House, looking for the fugitives.

Boscobel House.

Charles himself later recalled this event: 'In this wood I stayed all day without a meal or drink and by good fortune it rained all the time which hindered them, as I believe, from coming into the wood to search for men that might have fled there.'

Under cover of darkness Charles rode to Hobball Grange, near Tong, home to one of the five Penderel brothers, and from there to Evelith Mill, near Kemberton, where he and Penderel were forced to flee after they were challenged by the miller. After a meal the king was taken to Upper House in Madeley, the home of another staunch catholic with Royalist sympathies, Francis Wolfe, and was sheltered in the barn as it was deemed too dangerous to remain in the house. The barn is known today as 'King Charles' Barn'.

Wolfe and Penderel made their way to the River Severn to scout the nearby river crossings, but found them too well guarded by Parliamentary troops.

The next morning, 6 September, following their unsuccessful attempt to find a crossing over the River Severn, Penderel and Charles were forced to retrace their steps, this time making for another of the Gifford family's properties, Boscobel House, where they encountered another Royalist officer who had fought at Worcester, Colonel William Carless of Brewood.

The searching Roundhead patrols were everywhere and Charles, in company with Carless, spent all day hiding in a pollarded oak tree in Boscobel Wood, where they ate and drank the provisions they had been given. From their vantage point the pair could see Roundhead patrols searching the area. When it was deemed safe enough, Charles slept for a while in Carless' arms before spending that night in one of Boscobel's priest holes.

King Charles' Barn, Upper House, Madeley.

The Royal Oak at Boscobel.

From Boscobel the fugitives were taken by the five Penderel brothers across the Shropshire border to Moseley Old Hall, near Wolverhampton in Staffordshire, the home of Thomas Whitgreave who had fought and been wounded at the Battle of Naseby. They were forced to halt at Pendeford Mill, near Coven Heath, when the old horse Charles was riding was unable to continue. Two of the Penderel brothers continued on with Charles, in company with Francis Yates, arriving that evening at Moseley, where Thomas Whitgreave's Catholic priest, Father John Huddlestone, bathed the king's bleeding feet.

Charles stayed at Moseley for two days, hiding when required in the priest hole there (anyone visiting the Old Hall today can view the priest hole, and see how uncomfortable hiding there must have been). On 10 September, Parliamentary troops arrived and questioned Thomas Whitgreave, who managed to persuade them there was nothing suspicious there; the soldiers left without searching the house.

After that close call it was felt that staying at Moseley presented a risk not worth taking and so the king was taken to Bentley Hall, near Walsall, home of Colonel John Lane and his sister, Jane Lane, who they learned was in possession of a permit for herself and a servant to travel to Somerset to visit a pregnant friend,

Mrs George Norton of Abbot's Leigh in Somerset. Seeing an opportunity to get to Bristol, Charles agreed to pose as Jane Lane's servant.

When word came that no ships would be sailing from Bristol to France for a month, Charles continued on to the home of the Wyndham family in the village of Trent on the border with Dorset.

Despite many setbacks and narrow escapes along the south coast, Charles finally made a successful break for freedom. He and Lord Wilmot took a coal boat called *Surprise*, at a cost of £80 plus a later demand of £200 danger money, from Shoreham, near Brighthelmstone (Brighton) in Sussex to Fecamp, near Le Havre in France, landing on 16 October.

Charles Stuart spent the next nine years there until the restoration of the monarchy in 1660, following the death of Oliver Cromwell in 1658, and two years of political confusion.

The 'Monarch's Way' is a well-marked 625-mile footpath that traces the king's escape route from Worcester through south Shropshire and on eventually to Shoreham. The annual Royal Escape Yacht Race from Brighton to Fecamp commemorates Charles' escape.

The famous episode of the Royal Oak at Boscobel inspired the Oak Apple Day celebrations, and the name of numerous pubs called the Royal Oak. The original oak tree was so decimated by souvenir hunters that by 1712 it had been all but destroyed. The current royal oak was reputedly grown from an acorn from the original tree which was severely damaged in a storm in 2000.

BRIDGNORTH

~ *Bridgnorth's Funicular Railway* ~

Connecting Low Town to High Town, Bridgnorth's wonderful funicular cliff railway was opened on 7 July 1892 by the popular mayor John Anderson – popular because he declared a public holiday to celebrate the grand opening, construction having started in early November 1891. The cliff railway provided a more leisurely and easier assent to the top of the 100ft-plus-high sandstone cliff – not only the steepest inland funicular in the country, but also the oldest surviving, and arguably the shortest. The railway was advertised as 'a wonderful way to see the Severn Gorge and to partake of food and drink in the refreshment rooms or in the temperance restaurant'.

The cliff railway is one of four funiculars in the country, all built to the same basic design. On the north Devon coast is the Lynton and Lynmouth Cliff Railway; in Wales there is the Constitution Hill Railway in Aberystwyth; and in Bristol there is the Clifton Rocks Railway.

The engineer for the Bridgnorth funicular was Sir George Croydon Marks, first managing director of The Bridgnorth Castle Hill Railway Company Limited, registered in 1891, who was succeeded in that role by his brother, Edward Marks, from 1891 to 1924. Sir George was later created Lord Marks of Woolwich. Sir George's business partner, Sir George Newnes, the wealthy publisher, provided much of the original capital for the project. Newnes, chairman of the funicular between Lynton and Lynmouth, was the founder of the popular magazine-cum-newspaper *Tit-Bits*, as well as the famous *Strand Magazine* and *Country Life*, among many other publications.

Bridgnorth Cliff Railway was originally powered by a system of gravity and water until between 1943 and 1944, when the power system was changed to electricity. The length of the line is 201ft (61m); the height of travel is 111ft (34m); and there are two separate cars each on its own 3ft 6in gauge track.

Reputedly in 1830, for a wager, the eccentric Mad Jack Mitton rode a horse up the 185 (some say there are 200) Stoneway Steps at the side of the cliff railway, and on around the Castle Walk.

Bridgnorth's funicular cliff railway.

The alternative to the Cliff Railway for the more energetic amongst you is to wander (some say struggle) up the steep incline called the Cartway, which was the original route into High Town; stagecoaches needed six or eight horses to pull the coach up the steep slope.

~ *Tales of Buried Treasure* ~

In 1878, Bridgnorth found itself at the centre of a treasure hunt when groups of treasure hunters descended on Hermitage Hill. These erstwhile treasure seekers were chasing the legend that in one of the caves cut into the sandstone rock there was the entrance to an underground passage which led down through the earth to the River Severn, where they would find a large chest of gold. The tunnel was supposed to go under the River Severn and on to the Franciscan Friary on the west bank of the river. Another tunnel supposedly ran to a cave underneath Bridgnorth Castle. The caves are reputedly of Saxon origin, the first occupant being the grandson of King Alfred, Aethelard.

Up to the start of the Second World War, some of the caves were still used for habitation, the last family living there moving out in 1939.

Bridgnorth's seventeenth-century Town Hall, constructed from an old tithe barn.

The locals must have watched with much amusement as people dug away frantically, seeking the spot where the secret entrance lay. Enquiries as to its location would have been met with a shrug of the shoulders and a muttered response, for they knew there was no such entrance!

BROMFIELD

~ *The Crawler* ~

To the west of Ludlow, on the banks of the River Teme, near its confluence with the River Onny, stands the village of Bromfield. This was once the site of a grand manor house where there is a curious legend about a beautiful and headstrong heiress to the estate who, in the golden age of chivalry, met a gallant knight and fell deeply in love. Swept off her feet, she promised to marry him, and he in turn returned her love. Unfortunately, being a younger son, he was a landless knight. Sad to say, the maid's father, on hearing of the knight's lack of inheritance, strongly disapproved, and steadfastly refused to give his consent to the marriage. But his daughter dug in her heels, saying that she had sworn an oath to marry the knight, and that as she had given her word she would not be denied.

Outraged at his daughter's defiance of his decision, her father vowed that if she married the landless knight, her inheritance would not be one inch of his estate, but her marriage dowry would only be as much land as she could crawl over between sunset and sunrise.

Determined not to be cheated out of her dowry, the maid dressed herself in a pair of strong leather breeches, provided by an old family retainer to protect the delicate skin on her knees, and set off to defy her father. On that cold winter's night she managed to crawl around the fields, covering an area of 4 miles, and almost reaching the nearby village of Downton.

She returned to the house at sunrise, exhausted and covered in mud, just as her father was taking breakfast. She proudly told him what she had done, and claimed the land she had covered as her marriage dowry. Seeing the state of his daughter, her father's heart filled with pride at the courage of her indomitable spirit. He forgave her earlier defiance, and agreed to the marriage, naming her as his rightful heir.

Sadly only a few remains of the house exist on meadowland, however, the legend surrounding this place has endured – the field around which she crawled is reputedly known as 'Crawls', or 'Crawl Meadows'.

Bromfield is also the site of a Roman marching camp dating between AD 48–75. There were once in excess of twenty Bronze Age barrows or burial sites in the area, dating from 2,000 to 900 BC; sadly only three now survive.

BROSELEY

~ *The Broseley Jitties* ~

Approaching the turn of the seventeenth century, as the coalfields of Shropshire developed, the lord of the manor of Broseley, early industrialist James Clifford, provided small plots of land located at the edge of the town of Broseley in an area known as Broseley Wood. His aim was to attract immigrant workers, mostly miners, to the area, encouraged by the opportunity to build a cottage of their own. (Tradition had it that a man had a right to a house if he could erect a chimney and hearth in one day.)

Linking this jumble of cottages was a maze of narrow lanes and passageways known as the Broseley Jitties. The name given to each jitty described the people living there or its purpose, and included Balls Jitty; Carters Jitty; Coopers Jitty; Gittings Jitty; Goughs Jitty; Jews Jitty; Lloyds Jitty; Maiden's Jitty; Maypole Jitty; Mission Jitty; Plants Jitty; Pughs Jitty; and Simmonds Jitty. Tough and uncompromising people inhabited this irregular network of homes: people who reputedly lived in dire poverty and on the edge of society – and often beyond the law.

Alleyways in other places are referred to differently, for instance in Shrewsbury they are known as 'shuts', and in Yorkshire they are known as 'snickets'.

~ *Will You Take A Broseley?* ~

After Walter Raleigh made tobacco popular in England, smoking the dried leaves of the plant in clay pipes became increasingly favoured. Broseley was already a thriving centre of coal mining, and where there is coal it is usual to find clay and iron ore. Thus towards the end of the sixteenth century the manufacture of clay pipes blossomed in the town. There were three factories producing pipes in Broseley, at Bridge Bank, Benthall and Legg's Hill.

The question 'Will you take a Broseley?' became a familiar phrase in taverns and jitties.

The most famous Broseley maker of clay pipes was Richard Legg, whose 'churchwarden Pipe' was 25in long.

C

CHERRINGTON

~ The House that Jack Built ~

The well-known cumulative rhyme 'The House That Jack Built' first appeared in print in 1755, in the book *Nurse Truelove's New Year's-Gift, or The Book of Books for Children*. Randolph Caldecott's (1846–86) version was printed in 1878. The rhyme traces its origins to Shropshire, for Cherrington Manor, west of Newport, is fancifully claimed to be the inspiration for the poem, although there is no direct documentary evidence to back this claim up. Other views suggest that it originated from European folk tales, or from Jewish texts.

The rhyme begins with the line 'This is the house that Jack built', and goes on to tell us about the malt that lay in the house, the rat that ate it, the cat that ate the rat, and the dog that worried the cat, going on to tell us about the cow with the crumpled horn that tossed the dog, and the maiden all forlorn that milked the cow, then the judge all shaven and shorn that married the man all tattered and torn that kissed the maiden all forlorn. After this came a rooster, a farmer, and of course not forgetting a horse and hound.

The 1878 version was illustrated by Randolph Caldecott. He was born in Chester but spent a good deal of his early working life in Whitchurch as an employee of the Whitchurch and Ellesmere Bank. Known in literary circles as 'The Lord Of The Nursery', Caldecott's work transformed the world of children's books, which he published at the rate of two every Christmas, priced at 1 shilling per copy.

CHETWYND

~ They 'Ain't Getting' Me ~

Legend has it that in the eighteenth century one owner of Chetwynd Hall, north of Newport, was a curious sort, so much so that he sold the hall before the French Revolution because he was convinced the world was about to end. The truth is a little different.

The man in question was Robert Pigott (1736–94), who in 1770 inherited Chetwynd Hall on the death of his father, George Pigott, the hall having been in the family for three centuries.

Robert Pigott was not one for convention and grew to become a noted food and dress reformer. At Newmarket in 1770, Robert made a famous wager with the son of Sir William Codrington, of 500 guineas; the bet was that his father would outlive the other's. Not the most sensible flutter considering that his father, old Jacobite George Pigott, was at that time around 70 years of age, whereas Sir William was a mere 50 years old. A further complication arose when Robert Junior discovered that his father had in fact already died at Chetwynd some hours before the bet was made, at around 2 a.m., the bet being laid after dinner.

Robert Pigott refused to pay up, citing the fact that the prior death of his father nullified the bet. Young Codrington disagreed and demanded the bet be paid in full, and his assignee, Lord March, later the famous Duke of Queensbury, sued for the money. The case was brought before Lord Mansfield who, after considering all the evidence, declared that the impossibility of a contingency did not bar its becoming the subject of a wager, provided the impossibility is unknown to both parties at the time of laying it, and consequently gave judgement against Robert Pigott.

Four years later Robert Pigott was appointed to the office of High Sheriff of Shropshire, a post held previously by his grandfather. However, two years later, fearing that Britain was on the brink of disaster following the outbreak of the American War of Independence, Robert decided to sell his estates, including Chetwynd Hall, reportedly for the knock-down price of £70,000 – a steal considering the estate was worth £9,000 a year.

He became a strong supporter of the revolution in France, an ideal which he had become enraptured with. In 1791 Robert moved to the Continent, staying some time in Geneva and Lyons in Revolutionary France. He married a Frenchwoman, Margaret Henrietta Boutemps, in Geneva.

Robert Pigott was a highly principled man, a radical, and a vegetarian, who spoke out vociferously against the government, saying that England was not really free, and that the people had only a semblance of freedom. He was an advocator of the wearing of caps rather than tall hats, cocked or chimney-pot style. His argument was that these had been introduced by priests and despots, insisting that a cap allowed the face to be seen, and could have a variety of shapes and colours, whereas a hat was gloomy and morose. He was in Paris in 1792 when for a number of weeks the wearing of caps was all the rage. The Cap of Liberty (Le Bonnet Rouge) had been a symbol of the French Revolution from the outset, but it was Robert Pigott who promoted its wearing as an article of dress. As a zealous Pythagorean, as vegetarians were known as then, he advocated a vegetarian regime for prisoners, condemning the use of bread and instead recommending potatoes, lentils, maize, barley and rice. He was also a follower of the Scottish pioneer sex therapist, 'doctor' James Graham (he never finished medical school) and his electric celestial bed, which Graham claimed placed couples in the most advantageous position to conceive.

Robert Pigott died on 7 July 1794, in Toulouse, aged 58, having lived an exciting and varied life. His will states that he was a native of England, domiciled in the territory of the French Republic for about fifteen years, presently residing in the City of Toulouse, 55th Section, No. 436 in the Public Garden, and included the setting aside of the sum of 12,000 Livres for the construction of a mausoleum. He declared that he had four natural children: Charles Clegg Pigott and Marianne Clegg Pigott (both part French); and James Rousseau Stedman and Robert Stedman (both living in England).

~ *The Ghost of Madam Pigott* ~

Here's another tale about a ghostly spirit; this one involves an empty bottle and members of the Pigott family.

In the once-quiet village of Chetwynd, near Newport, in early 1800, the spirit of a lady by the name of Madam Pigott was a dreadful bugbear to the villagers in the area. Here's why: the Pigotts lived at Chetwynd Hall, and it seems that Madam Pigott, the wife of Squire Pigott, was not loved at all by her horrible husband. The word was that he had only married her to beget an heir to his estates and wealth. Soon after the marriage ceremony, he left her alone in the big house while he went off on a spree to carouse in the fleshpots of London, returning infrequently to the hall. After one of his visits, his lonely and neglected wife, desirous of his love and affection, fell pregnant. The frail woman was sickly throughout her pregnancy, spending much of her confinement in bed, where her feelings towards her rakish husband festered into bitterness.

At the time his wife went into labour the squire was in residence, on one of his rare visits to Chetwynd Hall. There were complications, and she was frail and lacking in strength. The doctor attending the birth explained the bad news that it was not possible to save both the lives of the mother and baby, asking what he should do. The cold-hearted squire reputedly ordered the doctor to concentrate his efforts on saving the child, and to allow his wife to die in childbirth, confirming that her husband was as callously indifferent to her in death as he had been towards her in life. The story goes that Madam Pigott overheard her husband's cold-hearted words, and cursed him as she gasped her final breath.

Sadly, the doctor was unable to save the child, and so both mother and baby died, but the angry spirits of both returned and were seen haunting the house and park, as well as the lanes towards Edgmond. There are places where the shades were more likely to be seen: at a twisted old tree root known as Madam Pigott's armchair; and at a high wall from which it was said she would leap down, together with her black cat, and cling fiercely to the back of any horseman stupid enough to ride past the spot at night. Not every rider was to be subjected to her torture. But if the person was riding to fetch help for a woman in childbirth, her malice was doubled.

At length a group of twelve clergymen joined forces to lay her ghost, as was the custom, by incessantly reading psalms and prayers out loud, but her power was too strong for them and her spirit refused to be laid. All but one of the priests, whose name was Foy, stubbornly carried on until he eventually managed to entice her spirit into a bottle, which was then sealed and flung into Chetwynd pool.

For a while life returned to normal, folks felt safe to walk around the lanes even at night, but unfortunately the peace was not to last. A child, who was skating on the ice that had formed on Chetwynd pool, broke the surface, and the bottle rose from the depths – releasing Madam Pigott's malevolent spirit on the local community once more. This time there was no Mr Foy to help lay her ghost for he had sadly died one winter, nonetheless twelve clergymen rallied to the cause and set about breaking her power. The priests chanted psalms and prayers until the spirit shrank in size, and finally, as before, her spirit entered the bottle, which was sealed rapidly. Having learned from previous experience, the bottle was not hurled into a body of water; this time it was taken to Newport cemetery, where it was buried under the chapel. Since then all has been calm and peaceful.

CHILD'S ERCALL

~ The Evil Eye ~

Since ancient times the evil eye has put a serious scare into people all around the world. Those that possessed this menace were seen to be a pariah on society, stigmatisation leading to ostracism. Suspicion fell on those with a squint, or anyone whose eyes were set at an uneven level. And if your eyebrows met, you had better watch out. It was also thought that someone with a physical deformity, or someone suspected of envying their neighbours possessed the evil eye.

Here's a curious story about a disagreeable farmer who once lived in the sleepy village of Child's Ercall, which lies some 6 miles south of Market Drayton. The farmer was feared by the local people because he was known to possess the evil eye, and because they suspected he was in league with the devil himself. He seemed to be able to control and manipulate the actions of any person who displeased him in any way.

On one particular day the farmer had popped into his local for a quiet drink when in waltzed a troop of Morris dancers, who proceeded to perform one of their boisterous dances. At the end of the dance one young Morrisman snatched up the farmer's half-full glass from the table he was sitting at and downed the foaming ale in one gulp. The farmer said nothing; all he did was look up into the young man's face, fixing him with an icy glare. The youth shrugged and followed his fellow dancers out into the yard, however, after only walking a short distance from the pub the lad juddered to a sudden halt, and stood rooted to the spot. Despite much encouragement from his chums the lad found himself unable to move. His fellow dancers, thinking he was playing some daft game, laughed at him then turned and walked away. Some considerable time passed before the youth found that his mobility had returned, but when he tried to go after his friends he found that his legs refused steadfastly to go in any other direction than back to the pub where the farmer was still sitting.

Once again the farmer fixed the youth with a chilling stare, and once again the lad found that he was unable to move. The farmer left his unhappy victim where he was until the following morning, when he finally released him. Apparently the young dancer fled from the pub as fast as his legs would carry him.

CHIRBURY

~ The Duelling Aristocrat ~

John Butler Edward Herbert, Lord Herbert of Chirbury (1582/83–1648), poet, soldier, adventurer, philosopher, linguist, lothario, noted duellist, and politician, was quite a guy. He was born in the house of his maternal grandmother, Lady Newport, in Eyton-upon-Severn, near Wroxeter, on 3 March 1582/83, the eldest son of Richard Herbert of Montgomery Castle, and Magdalen, daughter of Sir Richard Newport. The couple had six other sons plus three daughters.

Already having a good knowledge of Greek, Latin and logic, in May 1596, aged fourteen, Herbert attended University College, Oxford. A good horseman, and an excellent fencer, he taught himself French, Italian and Spanish, and found time to become proficient in music, particularly the playing of the lute. In 1600 he moved to London, presenting himself at Queen Elizabeth I's court, and three years later, in 1603, presented himself to the new king at Burghley House, Stamford, when James I was on his way to London. He was knighted by King James I on 24 July 1603. He returned to Montgomery Castle, and in 1606 was appointed Sheriff of Montgomeryshire.

A foreign tour with his friend, Aureilian Townsend, in the summer of 1608, saw him introduced to Paris high society, where he became acquainted with, and entertained by, the Grand Constable of France, Marguerite of Valois, the divorced wife of King Henry IV, and the Princess de Conti. During this period of his life he fought a number of duels, as well as acting as second in others.

He sailed for England from Dieppe, landing in Dover in February 1609, having narrowly escaped being shipwrecked on the voyage across the English Channel. But his restless nature took him back to the Continent as part of Edward Cecil's 4,000-strong force under Prince Christian of Anhalt, to besiege and recapture the town of Juliers. During the siege Herbert got into a drunken quarrel with Lord Theophilus Howard, challenging him to a duel, however, Edward Cecil managed to put a stop to this. He returned to England that September, where in his own words he described himself as being held 'in great esteem both in court and city', hinting that he could count Queen Anne (wife of King James I) amongst his army of admirers; there's no doubt he was popular among the ladies for there was a huge demand for copies of his portrait.

However, his next flirtation, this one with Lady Ayres, wife of Sir John Ayres, didn't work out too well, when in 1611 her husband found out, catching up with Herbert near Scotland Yard in London. Herbert was on the receiving end of a sound thrashing during which he was brutally stabbed.

For his next adventure he travelled around Europe, visiting Italy and France before making his way to the court of the Prince of Orange, arriving back in England in the winter of 1616/17. The next eighteen months saw him fight a number of duels, mostly as a result of petty arguments.

Lord Herbert was reputed to be a man of wide learning, of great wit and undoubted valour, plus he was a consummate egotist. His friendship with George Villiers, Earl of Buckingham, proved to be beneficial when he was offered the position of English Ambassador to France, and in October 1619 suggested to Buckingham that Princess Henrietta Maria of France would be a suitable bride for the young Prince, Charles Stuart (later King Charles 1). In 1621 Herbert was in trouble again, when he argued with and subsequently challenged Louis XIII's chief minister, Charles-Honore d'Albert, Duke de Luynes, the Constable of France, and the French king's favourite, to a duel. The duel was never fought because the duke, aged 43, died of a sudden fever whilst campaigning against the protestant Huguenots in Longueville. However, complaints against Herbert's behaviour saw him recalled.

When Herbert returned to England he was heavily in debt, his only reward an Irish peerage, Castleisland in County Kerry. But it wasn't until 7 May 1637 that he was finally raised to the English peerage when he was created Lord Herbert of Chirbury.

In 1632, Herbert commenced to write his history of the reign of King Henry VIII.

During the English Civil War, Lord Herbert was a half-hearted Royalist, staying as neutral as was possible, declining a summons from Prince Rupert to attend the king at Oxford on the grounds of ill health.

He surrendered Montgomery Castle to the Roundheads under Sir Thomas Middleton, desirous of avoiding the destruction of his library. The castle was subsequently besieged by Royalist forces, and on 17 September a battle was fought.

Herbert moved to his house in Queen Street, London, dying there on 20 August 1648.

CHURCH STRETTON

~ At the Court of King Caratacus ~

The lovely old market town of Church Stretton, nestling at the foot of the Long Mynd in the Stretton Hills in an area of outstanding beauty, is often called 'Little Switzerland'. A large hill to the eastern side of the A49 called Caer Caradoc is the disputed scene of a great battle.

The Chieftain of the Catuvellauni Tribe, 'Caradoc' in Welsh ('Caratacus' to the Romans), was a brave British leader who stood firm against the might of the Roman Empire. Caradoc's defiance culminated in the Battle of Caer Caradoc, in around AD 50, which took place on the slopes and summit of a hill described by the Roman historian Tacitus.

It is believed that prior to the battle Caradoc fled to South Wales after suffering a defeat in Kent at the hands of Aulus Plautius and his Roman hoard. There Caradoc persuaded the Silures Tribe to rebel, leading them back to Shropshire to fight the invading Romans. Caradoc used his knowledge to select what he believed to be a defendable position, namely at the top of Caer Caradoc. The Romans were commanded by Publius Ostorius Scapula.

Despite putting up a ferocious defence, Caradoc's relatively small force was no match against the superior strength and fighting organisation of the Roman Legions, and of course the Romans won. Caradoc managed to slip away, but his wife and children, together with his brother, were captured. Caradoc fled into the lands of the Brigantes Tribe, who were loyal to Rome. He was captured and treacherously handed over to the Romans by Queen Cartimandua of the Brigantes, and transported to Rome where he fully expected to be sentenced to death.

Paraded in chains through the streets of Rome, where news of his valour had preceded him, Caradoc held his head high, and was finally brought into the presence of the Emperor Claudius. It was there that he made a powerful speech of such eloquence and passion that on hearing it the emperor was persuaded to spare his life. He was pardoned and remained in Rome.

The site of the Battle of Caer Caradoc is disputed by many, who cite that Tacitus mentions in his description of the place that there was a body of water at the base of the hill, and of course Caer Caradoc has no such water at its base. Some claim that the battle took place at a spot in the Malvern Hills, others that it took place at Coxall Knoll, near Bucknell, Briedden Hill, or on Llanymynech Hill. And it should be remembered that there is another hill called Caer Caradoc in Shropshire, between Clun and Knighton. Wherever it was, it is one heck of a story.

CLUN

~ *The Dog Whipper* ~

People have resided in the area around Clun since prehistoric times, but its claim to fame is immortalised by A.E. Houseman in his work *A Shropshire Lad*. The Buffalo Inn in the town is where the romantic historical author Sir Walter Scott once stayed while writing *The Betrothed* and *The Talisman*, published jointly in June 1825 under the title *Tales of the Crusaders*, using Clun Castle as his model for the fortress 'Garde Douleureuse'. However, a century earlier the town's church was at the heart of a curious employment.

In 1741, it was recorded that the churchwarden at Clun was paid money for whipping unruly dogs from the building and grounds of the historic St George's

The ruins of eleventh-century Clun Castle.

The narrow fifteenth-century Packhorse Bridge at Clun which carries the A488 and the B4368 over the River Clun.

church. This practice existed between the sixteenth and nineteenth centuries, and was widespread across the country. The 'weapons' used by the churchwarden were a 3ft-long whip, plus a pair of dog tongs. Any cheeky animal following their owners to church or simply just wandering in off the lane would be shooed away or grabbed before they could get anywhere near the communion bread and wine, or, as in some reported cases, biting worshipers and fighting with other dogs.

It was not unknown for the dog whipper to use his whip on worshipers who had the nerve to fall asleep during the service. For instance, in 1659 in Claverley, a Christian gentleman by the name of Richard Dovey bequeathed property near All Saints' church with the caveat that 8 shillings of the annual rent was paid to the dog whipper, to awaken sleepers and to discourage sluggards, as well as driving out dogs. There is no mention of other animal species being in need of such a control method.

~ *The Day the Earth Moved* ~

At 1.46 p.m. and 34.2 seconds UTC (Universal Time Coordinated) on 2 April 1990, much of England and Wales experienced a powerful earth tremor, the epicentre of which geologists finally concluded was in the Shropshire village of Clun (the ancient geological Pontesbury–Linley fault line lies nearby). This sudden movement in the fault sent shockwaves reverberating vast distances across the country: Kent in the south-east, Cornwall in the south-west, Newcastle upon Tyne in the north-east, and even the Republic of Ireland all felt the shockwaves.

Damage to buildings was reported in Clun, Wrexham and Shrewsbury, with people being evacuated from homes and shops, and electrical power was disrupted after transformers in substations tripped out. The earthquake even caused some damage to Clun Castle and some minor damage was also recorded in Liverpool and Manchester. The tremor, which lasted around 15 to 30 seconds, was initially measured at between 4.9 and 5.4 on the Richter Scale, its final recorded magnitude being set at 5.1, making it the strongest earthquake in the UK since the 5.4 Llyn Peninsular Quake in Gwynedd, North Wales on 19 July 1984.

Earthquakes are not unknown on the border between England and Wales: Hereford experienced sizable quakes in 1896, and again in 1924. There was a tremor near Ludlow in 1926, and another near Shrewsbury in 1932.

COALBROOKDALE

~ The First Ironman ~

Coalbrookdale sits on the high wooded banks of the River Severn in what we know today as the Ironbridge Gorge. This place bore witness to the birth of the Industrial Revolution, which changed a beautiful, peaceful spot into one of furnaces and factories. Two centuries ago scores of men, women, girls and boys toiled tirelessly here in sweltering conditions, amidst a pall of stinking fumes and pollution that hung over the entire area. Now the Ironbridge Gorge is a UNESCO World Heritage Site, housing many museums dedicated to our industrial past. It is a place where the reputations of many titans of the Industrial Revolution were forged, among them a Cumberland-born man by the name of John Wilkinson (1728–1808).

It was here on the River Severn at Coalbrookdale in 1787 that the world's first iron boat, *The Trial*, was built and launched. Responsible for this historical breakthrough was John 'Iron Mad' Wilkinson, pioneer of working with iron, and manufacturer of many products, including cannons, mortars, and shell casings. Wilkinson's problem was how to move these very heavy items from the factory to the customer. His solution was to ship the goods down the River Severn, but there was no way that the slim-hulled, shallow draught prows that sailed the river could carry the weight required, so John built a boat made of iron specially for this purpose, thus solving his transport problems as well as starting a whole new era in ship design.

The iron boat was 70ft long, with a beam of 6ft 8½in, and it weighed 8 tons, with a capacity of 32 tons. It was launched from Willey Wharf on 6 July 1787. Unfortunately the idea of iron boats did not catch on and *The Trial* later became known as *John's Folly*.

The bottom of the Hay Inclined Plane connecting the Coalport Canal to Blists Hill, Coalbrookdale.

John Wilkinson was born in the village of Little Clifton, Bridgefoot, Cumberland (Cumbria). His father, Isaac, was employed as a pot-founder at a local blast furnace. Educated in Kendal, in 1745 John was apprenticed for five years to a Liverpool merchant before entering into a partnership with his father at Bersham furnace near Wrexham.

In 1757, a blast furnace was built at Willey, near Broseley. Wilkinson also established iron works at Hollinswood, Snedshill, Hadley and Hampton Loade, and in partnership with Edward Blakeway leased land at Bradley, near Wolverhampton, where another iron works was built.

John married Ann Maudesley in 1755, and relocated his home to Broseley, and named it The Lawns.

As well as being one of the major partners in the construction of the world's first iron bridge, John Wilkinson was a prolific inventor and patented a number of techniques such as boring machines for cannons and cylinders of steam engines.

The Lawns, Broseley, once the home of ironmaster John Wilkinson.

He died on 14 July 1808, and was buried in a coffin made of iron at Lindale, Cumbria, a part of his Castlehead estate, but was subsequently moved a number of times; sadly the location of his final resting place has been lost in the mists of time.

~ *Ether Anyone?* ~

Ironmaster John Wilkinson suffered a great deal from ill health, particularly in 1796 when he was in great pain from an undescribed physical complaint. During that time the great man was wrestling with the problems associated with the development of a new shingling hammer, and a new method of rolling. By late 1797, his condition had become so serious that he was advised to take some time off. By Christmas, Wilkinson was gravely ill, his only relief coming from Mrs Price's patent cure. Fortunately he recovered by taking copious quantities of ether.

The taking of Diethyl Ether with its anaesthetic and intoxicating effects was widespread in the 1700s, both as a medical treatment and as a recreational drug. A clear liquid with a strong dense smell was applied as an oil for ailments such as toothache, earache, headache and pains in the neck, and was often used as a substitute for alcohol. Taken in small doses, it resulted in a state of euphoric intoxication by rapidly depressing the central nervous system. It was usual for the user to drink between 1oz and 3oz of the liquid drug.

Ether was also relatively cheap and did not result in a hangover. It was taken orally, on sugar lumps or mixed with wine. It was also considered good at aiding relief from a wide range of conditions such as lethargy, epilepsy, whooping cough, hysteria, syncope (swooning or fainting) and pains in the chest. Dr Thomas Beddows published a paper in 1794, stating the benefits of the inhalation of ether.

In Ireland in the 1880s, the drinking of ether was a way to get drunk after taking the pledge to give up alcohol (abstinence was strongly promoted by the Catholic Church). Drinking ether was also popular in Scotland, Norway, France and Russia, and amongst Polish peasants.

CONDOVER

~ *Alas, Poor Yorrick* ~

The character of Yorrick, the court jester in William Shakespeare's *Hamlet*, was apparently based upon a real person: Richard Tarlton of Condover near Shrewsbury, Queen Elizabeth I's jester. The story goes that Prince Hamlet finds the dead jester's skull when two gravediggers are scooping out earth for a new grave in which to bury poor Ophelia, and says those immortal lines, 'Alas, poor Yorrick. I knew him, Horatio. A fellow of infinite jest.'

No one knows for certain when Richard Tarlton (sometimes spelled Tarleton) was born; some have stated the date as being 1530, others sometime in the 1550s, and to be fair there is more than a little speculation regarding the actual place of his birth. His father's name remains a mystery, however, we are told that his mother's name was Katherine, and that he had a sister by the name of Helen, and that at some point the family relocated to Ilford in Essex.

The most accepted account of Tarlton's life was written by English churchman and historian Thomas Fuller who in his book *History of the Worthies of England*, published in 1662, gave an account of how Tarlton became a jester. It tells of his rise from humble beginnings to the pinnacle of Elizabethan fame. Apparently one day young Tarlton was working in the fields taking care of his father's pigs when the servant of Robert Dudley, Earl of Leicester, came by en route to the earl's lands in Denbigh. Engaging in conversation, the servant was so pleased with the wit of Tarlton's 'happy/unhappy' reposts that he took the young man to court, where he became Queen Elizabeth I's favourite jester.

Theatrical success with various troops of roving actors, including Sussex's Men in the 1580s and The Queen's Men in 1583, at the Curtain Theatre in London, increased Tarlton's fame and status, as borne out by the fact that Sir Philip Sidney was godfather to Tarlton's son, Philip.

Reports claim that Tarlton once made the queen laugh so much that she had him removed from the stage. He made jokes about the queen's royal favourites including Sir Walter Raleigh and Robert Dudley, but took them too far and fell out of favour.

As a comedic actor, Tarlton was known for his extempore comic doggerel verse, which became known as 'Tarltons'. He was an accomplished dancer and musician, and a master of fencing – he was an excellent swordsman. He was also a writer, composer of ballads, jigs and pamphlets, and at least one full length play titled *The Seven Deadly Sins*. Aside from the character Yorrick, Tarlton is also said to have been Shakespeare's inspiration for the character Bottom in *A Midsummer Night's Dream*.

Richard Tarlton died of the plague in 1588, supposedly still in his late 30s – a legend in his own lifetime – and is buried in St Leonard's churchyard, Shoreditch, London.

Years after Tarlton's death, a book of his jests was published posthumously in three parts: *His Courtly Witty Jests*; *His Sound City Jests*; and *His Country Pretty Jests* (a sort of Elizabethan version of Bob Monkhouse's famous joke book), which were described as being full of delight, wit and honest mirth.

COUND

~ Let the Mountain Come to Mohamed ~

Early in the 1800s, the *Shrewsbury Chronicle* reported a rather curious incident regarding a meeting that took place near Shrewsbury post office, when the owner of Cound Mill, John Cressett Pelham of Cound Hall, told factory owner and ironmaster William Hazledine that he wanted him to demolish Cound Mill and rebuild it closer to the water source that drove the waterwheel, and would he get on with the work.

A perplexed Hazledine queried the request, countering with the logical argument that it would be much more practical to divert the water source than to knock down the existing mill buildings. However, the ever eccentric Pelham flatly refused to listen to Hazledine's advice and told him so, to which Hazledine replied that he didn't want the job.

Both men left the scene continuing to shout at one another, and did not speak again for eighteen months until one day Pelham strolled unannounced into Hazledine's office. Calmly, Pelham asked Hazledine to undertake the job at Cound as previously outlined, to which the ironmaster nodded his ascent. The work was subsequently carried out, at the cost of many hundreds of pounds, without another word passing between them.

D

DIDDLEBURY

~ The Unsinkable Molly Morgan ~

Convict and landowner, Molly Morgan (1762–1835) was born in the village of Diddlebury, between Bridnorth and Ludlow, where she was baptised Mary Jones on 31 January 1762. Her father, David Jones, was employed as a ratcatcher, and her mother was Margaret Jones, *née* Powell. When young Molly, as she liked to call herself, left school she became a dressmaker, and on 25 June 1785, aged 22, she married wheelwright and carpenter William Morgan of Hopesay. Their union was blessed with two children.

All went well until four years later, when Molly was caught stealing hempen yarn from a bleaching factory. Her husband was also charged, but he escaped from gaol and fled. Molly was tried at Shrewsbury Assizes on 8 August 1789, found guilty, and sentenced to transportation to Australia for seven years.

St Peter's church, Diddlebury.

The infamous hell-ship *Neptune* of the Second Fleet was the vessel Molly and over 500 other convicts had the misfortune to embark on 28 June 1790. More than half the number of prisoners aboard the overcrowded ship either died at sea or soon after arriving in Port Jackson, Sydney Harbour, Botany Bay. In contrast, Molly arrived in fine fettle, having swapped favours with a number of the ship's officers in exchange for better treatment and rations.

Will Morgan was eventually recaptured and he, too, was transported to Australia, where he and Molly were reunited in old Sydney Town where she worked in a female factory, and he on labour gangs. After a period of good behaviour, Molly gained a ticket-of-leave licence (parole), and the couple opened up a little shop.

Sadly Molly seems to have become bored and fallen out of love with Will, who quarrelled with her because of her constant flirting and finally dumped her. Undeterred, Molly became mistress to Captain John Locke of the store ship *Resolution*, and on 9 November 1794, along with thirteen other convicts, she escaped and travelled to England on the ship when it left for England. Locke proposed marriage but Molly declined his offer, and upon arrival in England made her way to Plymouth, where she met and bigamously married Thomas Mears, a wealthy brassfounder.

Tragedy wasn't far off and in 1803, when their home mysteriously burnt down, Mears accused Molly of the crime. She was arrested and tried on 10 October 1803 at Croydon Sessions, where she was found guilty and sentenced to transportation.

She arrived back at Port Jackson in Australia on 24 June 1804, aboard the ship *Experiment*. Unable to find her husband, Will Morgan, she acquired various protectors, among them a man named Thomas Byrne, but several years later after being granted a piece of land and a few cattle Molly once again found herself in trouble with the authorities. Her tiny herd of cattle had mysteriously and rapidly grown in size, causing the local government officials to grow suspicious of her farming methods. It transpired that the ingenious Molly had been rustling free-grazing government cattle and branding them as her own.

This time Molly's good looks and abundant charms didn't help and she was sentenced to seven years in Newcastle Penal Colony, Australia, the place where the most wicked convicts were sent. However, it didn't take her long to find a new protector amongst the overseers, and three years later, in 1819, she was one of a handful of well-behaved prisoners to be granted a ticket-of-leave by the Governor, and sent to the settlement of Wallis Plains, where she was again given some land.

Success as a farmer ensued, and she opened a legal wine shanty, calling the grog shop the Angel Inn. In 1822 she married Thomas Hunt, an Army Officer stationed at the local garrison. In 1823, the Governor was so impressed with her success that he sanctioned her leasing 159 acres, and agreed to her using a convict clearing gang.

The mid-1820s saw Molly a rich woman who gave generously to the poor. In 1828, she was recorded as being one of the largest landowners on the Hunter River. Sadly, Molly, 'The Queen of the Hunter River', still vivacious in her dotage and whose life story would surely grace any Hollywood blockbuster, died on 27 June 1835, aged 73.

DITHERINGTON

~ A World First ~

Ditherington Flax Mill, in what is now a suburb of Shrewsbury, is the world's first skyscraper, although it must be remembered that this descriptive term had not yet been thought up. The 7-acre plot of land on which the mill was to be built was owned by the Benyon brothers. Work on the building started in 1796 and was completed in 1797, by business partners John Marshall of Leeds, and brothers Thomas and Benjamin Benyon, plus Charles Bage. This four-tier building pioneered the use of iron-frame construction. The estimated cost of the construction was around £17,000, (almost £1 million in today's money), including all the mill equipment. The investors had seen the opportunity to build a mill to twist thread to sell to nearby carpet weavers in Kidderminster and Bridgnorth.

John Marshall was the owner of a flax-spinning mill in Leeds, a venture into which, in 1793, the two Benyon brothers, born near Whitchurch, reportedly invested around £9,000 (over £500,000 today). The Benyons were in the woollen trade, buying and selling Welsh cloth, which they stored in their Mardol warehouse; a business so profitable that by 1786 they were partners in a bank.

In 1795, the partnership built a mill in Water Lane, Leeds, which on 13 February 1796 burned down. From contemporary accounts it would appear that the relationship between the three men was not always harmonious. That said, following the fire the Benyons persuaded Marshall to build a new fire-proof mill on a plot of land they owned at Ditherington.

The metalwork for the building was cast at the Coleham factory of Shawbury-born William Hazledine, including columns, beams, roof sections, tie-bars, staircases, windows and doors, plus many other items.

The designer/architect chosen for the Ditherington project was Derby-born Charles Woolley Bage (1751–1822), a wine and liquor merchant and surveyor – an odd combination of expertise. However, Bage was an enthusiastic advocate of the uses of iron, and a disciple of William Strutt, a pioneer in this method of construction. Bage, born a Quaker, also went on to build the world's third and eighth iron-framed buildings. His family moved to Elford in Staffordshire shortly after he was born, where his father founded a papermill before investing in an ironworks in partnership with others, one of whom was the fellow Quaker Erasmus Darwin, grandfather of Charles Darwin. He was also a friend of Robert Darwin, the great man's father.

Charles Bage married a Shrewsbury girl, Margaret Boterall, and the couple set up home in Shrewsbury in 1781. As a young man Bage had become interested in the application of iron technology in construction, and gas technology in lighting, and in later life he also found time to become a novelist.

The partnership in Ditherington Mill was dissolved in 1804, after relationships between Marshall and the Benyons deteriorated, with John Marshall buying out the others at an enormous sum of £70,000 (approaching £4 million today). At that time the mill was valued at £64,000. Utilising the money from the sale of Ditherington, the other partners then built a mill of their own at Castlefields, Shrewsbury, again to Bage's design. In 1807, Bage was elected Mayor of Shrewsbury, and in 1813 helped with the establishment of the charity Lancasterian School, which he also designed. When his first wife died in 1808, Bage, aged 56, married a 21-year-old, and together they produced a brood of six children.

In 1811, a fire destroyed part of the mill at Ditherington. In 1815, Bage built a small linen weaving factory on what today is Burr's field, but the business was not successful.

Britain was deep in an economic depression in 1815, continuous wars had plunged the country into deficit, the national debt was around £800 million, and against this climate many businesses suffered. Bage, in a letter to William Strutt, set out his fears for the country, predicting the rise of the infant country of the United States of America, who would be 'a giant great enough to swallow up almost the rest of the world' – how right he was. Sadly, apart from a street named after him – Bage Way – Bage's only monument is his gravestone in St Chad's churchyard.

Ditherington Flax Mill closed in 1886, and the property was sold for the low sum of £3,000, including a bleach yard in Hanwood. The mill was subsequently converted to a maltings by William Jones Maltsters Limited, until that company was declared bankrupt in 1934. In the Second World War the site was used as a barracks for the Light Infantry, and later by brewers Ansells until its final closure in 1987.

The Benyon brothers died in quick succession: Thomas in 1833, and Benjamin in 1834. Benyon Street is named after them.

What of John Marshall? Well, despite the country's financial problems, his fortunes continued in the ascendency: in 1821 he was Sheriff of Cumberland; and in 1826 he was elected MP for Yorkshire. However, three years later ill health forced him to resign his seat and retire to his Watermillock estate on the shores of Ullswater in the Lake District. His fortune was estimated at between £1.5 and £2.5 million.

E

EDGMOND

~ Feng Shui versus Superstition ~

Here's a strange superstition which doubtless must have been repeated in many other places across the country, not just in the Shropshire village of Edgmond. It is surely one of the first examples of the art of Feng Shui in England. It concerns the position of furniture in a room – in the case of this particular superstition, the bedroom. Here in Edgmond in the nineteenth century it was apparently a matter of great importance to have one's bed positioned in the correct manner. The main consideration is that it must be sympathetic with the other woodwork of the bedroom. To do otherwise may have grave consequences, and here's why. Superstition had it that if a bed was positioned across the floorboards rather than in line with them, then this would prevent sleep. Another superstition in a similar vein was that if a dying woman's bed was placed under a cross-beam supporting the roof then she would suffer great agony because her spirit would be unable to find release.

As an illustration of this consequence I offer the following: residing in Edgmond in the 1800s was a wealthy young woman who one day directed her servants to rearrange the furniture in her bedroom – nothing to get in a sweat about, or so one might think. However, when she explained how she wanted them to site the bed they flatly refused to do her bidding, saying that if it were placed across the floorboards then there would follow an almighty calamity in the form of a death in the family. The mistress of the house dug her heels in and ordered the servants to carry out her wishes which, wanting to keep their jobs, they did.

Uh oh! You guessed it. Three months later an elderly lady relative of the woman died. The servants believed this to be the fulfilment of their prophecy. The fact that the deceased was very old had nothing to do with it, of course.

ELLESMERE

~ A Mere Story ~

The town of Ellesmere lies at the heart of Shropshire's very own Lake District, with its proliferation of meres and mosses. There are many legends surrounding

The mere at Ellesmere, the largest of the nine glacial meres in the Shropshire 'Lake District'.

the question of how Ellesmere's great mere was formed. This particular story first requires you to forget all of science's reasoning of retreating glaciers at the end of the last Ice Age, and instead to take heed of the folklore surrounding this immense body of water. Legend has it that the mere was formed when an old woman locked up her well to prevent her neighbours from using it. Guess what happened? Yep, the well overflowed, in the process drowning the mean old woman and thus formed the mere. It's as simple as that.

An interesting fact about the area is that during the early part of the Second World War, between 1940 and 1941, Gadlas Hall, near Ellesmere, provided sanctuary for General Charles de Gaul and his family.

~ *More Mere Legends* ~

Not many people know that there is another legend about the mere; this one involves Asrais – a species of gentle water fairy, who live in the deep dark depths of Ellesmere's mere. These benevolent creatures only rise to the surface once every hundred years, to see the moon, so it is no surprise that no one has ever witnessed this ritual.

There is a curious story of a fisherman who one day was out fishing on the mere and accidentally caught an Asrai. He was so intrigued with his catch, he determined to show off the beautiful fairy to his friends and relations, and so he tried to take her home with him; unfortunately, as soon as she was touched by the sun's rays she melted into foam.

The sad piscatorial lost his prized catch, but in one sense he was lucky, because the beautiful, gentle Asrais are not the only things lurking below the surface of the mere – there is another of a much more sinister nature, as a poor Ellesmere angler discovered when he chose to disobey the golden rule that one should not go fishing on a Sunday. His catch proved to be the worst he could make, for he caught the devil himself. Old Satan was not best pleased to be so disturbed and dragged the fisherman from his boat down into the murky depths – he was never seen again.

EYTON

~ The Stupid Robber ~

The tiny settlement of Eyton, lying between Baschurch and Myddle, was once the scene of a horrendous murder. The perpetrator was a man by the name of Hugh Elks. He had learned that there was a considerable sum of money kept at the home of a resident of Eyton, and he was determined to relieve that person of it. Elks chose to commit the crime when the house owners would be attending Sunday-morning service, figuring that the house would be deserted. He gathered together a few fellow criminals and set off with them and his faithful dog to rob the house. As a precaution, before entering the house they pulled visors over their faces to mask their identities, however, the house was not completely deserted for when they entered they found a servant girl making cheese. Elks sat her down and stooped to bind her, but as he did so she saw his face under the visor. Recognising him, she is reputed to have called him Uncle Elks, and begged him to do her no harm. Her plea went unheard as Elks pulled out his knife and slit the girl's throat. His fellow thieves, horrified at what he had done, took fright and fled from the house back to Baschurch, empty handed. Elks, seeing his companions desert him, chased after them, in his haste slamming the door shut behind him. Unfortunately for Elks he had inadvertently shut his dog in the house. Elks went first to Marton and from there ran to the church at Petton, entering shortly before the end of the service.

When the rest of the Eyton household returned from church, they were horrified to discover the dead girl and Elks' dog, almost bursting from eating all the cheese. The dog was allowed to leave, and was followed to the home of Hugh Elks, who was then apprehended on suspicion of murder. The coroner's inquest was convened for the following day, and Elks was arraigned, still protesting his innocence, claiming that at the time of the murder he was attending the church service at Petton.

Unfortunately for Elks a witness, a maid servant who worked at a house in Marton, testified that she had heard the town-gate at Marton bang shut and had looked through a window to see what had caused it – Hugh Elks coming from the gate at around a time corresponding to the middle of the service. Elks refuted the maid's claim, saying that it would be impossible to see the town-gate from any window in that house. The coroner then had the entire jury taken from Eyton to Marton, whereupon the maid showed them the window which indeed had an excellent view of the gate in question. The jury therefore pronounced him guilty, and he was sent to Shrewsbury for trial, where he was found guilty of murder and subsequently hanged.

F

FORD

~ The Custom of Heaving ~

Reputedly on Easter Monday in the late 1800s in the small Shropshire village of Ford, near Shrewsbury, two young women who were strangers to the area came upon a sizeable party of men carrying a decorated chair. Of course the women were a bit apprehensive, especially when the men approached them, and even more so when the men insisted on 'heaving' them before they would let them pass.

So what exactly is the curious custom of heaving? In the nineteenth and early twentieth centuries, the custom of heaving was widespread throughout the county of Shropshire. It was a popular custom which on Easter Monday involved the boys heaving the girls, whilst on Easter Tuesday the girls would heave the boys. The person to be heaved was placed in the chair, which was decorated with ribbons, flowers and foliage, then raised high into the air.

In keeping with many other traditions, the origins of this custom are more than a little obscure. Many believe that it is a pagan ritual linked to Eostre's Throne of Spring, celebrating the arrival of the spring equinox; Eostre was a Goddess, sometimes known as Ostara, after whom the springtime Paschal (Passover) festival is named. There is another belief that the ritual symbolises the resurrection of Christ.

Another example can be found in the story of a young military officer in north Shropshire who, one Easter Tuesday in the early 1900s, was on his way to dine with a neighbour. His walk was rudely interrupted at the gates of his neighbour's home by a party of women toting a chair. He promised them money in an attempt to buy them off, but they refused. Instead, and without further ado, they grabbed him and proceeded to heave him. Then they carried him up the carriage drive and set him down at his friend's door, before going on their merry way to find another unsuspecting man.

Citizens of a more nervous disposition were known to go a long distance out of their way to avoid being heaved, although there were many who are reported to have enjoyed the experience.

For instance there was once a man, a resident of the Talbot Hotel in Shrewsbury, who on Easter Tuesday was quietly eating his breakfast when a gang of boisterous female servants of the hotel waltzed into the breakfast room toting a chair decorated with white ribbon. The man was seated in the chair and hoisted high, and before they would release him the ladies demanded a ransom in return for a kiss. This sort of heaving behaviour was reputedly common amongst the maids of hotels, and female servants of large private houses.

The custom of heaving seems to have died out before the First World War – sad really because it sounds like a lot of fun. However, I have heard of recent efforts to revive the tradition, so all may not be lost.

G

BOLAS MAGNA OR GREAT BOLAS?

~ Sad-Faced Harry ~

This is a story that would be more at home at the heart of a romantic novel. In the eighteenth century in the small peaceful village of Bolas Magna, also known as Great Bolas, there lived a beautiful young lady by the name of Sarah Hoggins, the daughter of the local miller Thomas Hoggins. The village lies a few miles north-west of Newport, where two Shropshire rivers, the Tern and the Meese, meet.

A newcomer to the village at that time was an itinerant worker, a sad-faced man of good manners and obvious education, who was employed by Thomas Hoggins, and as a consequence came to know the beautiful Sarah. To protect his real identity he had given his name as John Jones, but actually his name was Harry, and Harry had a big secret, something which only the local vicar knew: Harry's true name was Henry Cecil, and he was no wandering itinerant worker, he was in fact Lord Burghley, heir to the Earl of Exeter.

Harry was married to Emma Vernon, a wealthy heiress, the daughter of Thomas Vernon of Hanbury Hall, in Worcestershire. After their marriage in 1776, the couple moved into Hanbury Hall, where Harry spent his time modernising and updating the house and its estates. Later in 1776, Emma gave birth to a child, who sadly died aged just two months. However, despite having a healthy income, the couple fell into debt.

Things went wrong in 1785, when Emma met the new curate of Hanbury church, the Reverend William Sneyd, with whom she fell in love, and the couple began an affair. In May 1789, Emma confessed her love for the clergyman and begged Harry to allow her to live with Sneyd, which he refused. She pleaded to be allowed one last meeting with the object of her affection, to which Harry agreed, taking her to Birmingham for the supposed last meeting. But Emma betrayed her husband and eloped with the curate, leaving Harry to return to Hanbury broken-hearted.

Harry left his estates in the hands of a friend, with the instruction to gather in rents due to pay off his debts, and left Hanbury in search of a quiet life. He wandered the land until he arrived at Bolas Magna in June 1789, where he found refuge.

Calling himself John Jones, he purchased a small cottage and began life as an itinerant worker.

Initially, 16-year-old Sarah Hoggins took pity on the sad man working for her father, but her feelings for him grew stronger each day, and he began to cheer as he also fell in love. The pair married in St John the Baptist's church in Bolas Magna in April 1790, Harry still using the name John Jones, for what in truth was a bigamous marriage. Harry subsequently obtained a divorce from the Consistory Court, and an Act of Parliament pronounced him able to re-marry.

The happy couple were married for a second time on 3 October 1791, at St Mildred's church in Bread Street, London. Harry had purchased some land in Bolas Magna and had a small house built, known as Bolas Villa. The pair lived a simple life in what is now Burleigh Farm.

When his uncle, the Ninth Earl, died in 1793, Harry inherited the title of 10th Earl of Exeter, and in 1801 was created 1st Marquess of Exeter. He and Sarah, now Marchioness of Exeter, moved to Burghley House, near Stamford in Lincolnshire, passing the ownership of Bolas Villa to his godson, Cresswell Tayleur.

Alfred Lord Tennyson wrote a poem about their love story, *The Lord of Burleigh*. Unfortunately it's not one of his best, and he even changed sad-faced Harry's employment to that of a landscape-painter, presumably just to make the text rhyme.

Unfortunately this story does not have a happy ending. Sarah died, aged 23, on 18 January 1797, giving birth to her fourth child, the eldest of which is buried at Great Bolas. After Sarah's death Henry (Harry) Cecil remarried, and he died in 1804, aged 50.

GREAT NESS

~ Bandits Galore ~

For centuries, the pass at Great Ness was a popular place for highwaymen and bandits, who used Nesscliffe Hill as a lookout post. They were looking to spot plump merchants travelling to and from Shrewsbury, who regularly journeyed to Oswestry market to purchase good quality Welsh cloth to sell to Shrewsbury tailors to make clothes. Of necessity the merchants had to carry large quantities of gold and silver with which to buy the goods. Travelling between Shrewsbury and Oswestry was hazardous at the best of times, because they had to pass the high wooded hill known as Nesscliffe, the high road running through a narrow pass which was the perfect place for an ambush. From their high vantage point on the hill, bandits would keep a sharp eye out for baggage trains, and swoop down to relieve the poor travellers of their cash and goods.

Nearby, a little way to the east, was a notorious inn known as the Wolf's Head (now a private house), which was the haunt of many of these outlaws who would gather there to brag about their exploits. One such outlaw was the infamous highwayman Sir Humphrey Kynaston.

Many tales abound about Sir Humphrey and his fiery steed Beelzebub. One rather fanciful legend has it that Sir Humphrey once jumped his horse from the top of Nesscliffe Hill, landing in Ellesmere, a leap of only 9 miles – such is the stuff of legends.

H

HOPTON CASTLE

~ The Scene of Great Butchery ~

Hopton Castle, a medieval tower house near Aston-on-Clun, was the scene of one of the English Civil War's most brutal events. The castle was like a weekend retreat for wealthy Walter de Opton (later de Hopton) and his family in the thirteenth century, a kind of holiday home in the country.

In 1644, Hopton Castle was the property of staunch Parliamentarian Robert Wallop (a judge at the trial of King Charles I, although not a signatory to Charles' death warrant). Lieutenant Wright of Brampton Bryan Castle arranged for Hopton Castle to be manned by a small garrison before it could be grabbed by Royalist forces. Various Royalist attacks were made, and over time the garrison was increased to thirty-one Parliamentary soldiers under the command of Samuel More. In early March, faced with a vast army of Royalists under the command of Sir Michael Woodhouse, the Parliamentary defenders held out valiantly for around

The ruins of Hopton Castle.

five weeks. Woodhouse made more than one demand for More to surrender the castle, but each time it was refused. The final Royalist demand was accompanied by the threat that failure to surrender would result in no quarter being given.

Finally, in dire straits, More asked to be allowed to march away the garrison, retaining their arms, and when this was refused by the Royalist commander, More sued for the lives of his men. When More finally surrendered the garrison, he was taken away for questioning. His men, however, were not so fortunate. Instead of being imprisoned, twenty-eight of them had their throats cut and their bodies were thrown into the moat.

Following the restoration of Charles II, Robert Wallop was imprisoned and died in the Tower of London in 1667. Colonel More later became the military leader of Parliamentary forces in Shropshire, Governor of Montgomery Castle, Governor of Ludlow Castle and Hereford, and later a Member of Parliament.

I

⸎ IRONBRIDGE ⸎

~ The Girl in the Pit ~

On Saturday, 30 March 1822, 22-year-old Samuel Johnson was executed at Shrewsbury for the rape and murder of Mary Sandfod, an 18-year-old woman in the district of Ironbridge, on 3 March 1822.

At his trial the jury was told that despite being married, Johnson was so attracted to the girl that he seldom missed a night without paying her a visit to pay his respects, paying her every attention. He invited her to accompany him to a dance which was to take place on Wednesday evening, to which she readily agreed. However, on that fateful evening, as they set off, Johnson told her that he was not feeling well, but with her agreement they would carry on walking across the fields.

In 1779 the world's first iron bridge was erected over the River Severn in Shropshire, and is today Britain's best-known industrial monument.

Mary objected, saying that if he could not go to Ironbridge then she would return home as she expected a female friend to call at her house that evening.

Even so the couple continued to walk across the fields for some distance, and then were seen no more, until Johnson met James Smith, a labourer, with whom he was acquainted. Smith testified that he had asked Johnson where he had been so late. According to Smith, Johnson replied in a rough manner, 'I have been nowhere', before hurrying on at a quick pace.

It transpired that when Johnson and Miss Sandfod were some distance from any house, he had proceeded to use the young woman in a most brutal manner. The marks left on the ground by her feet and the signs of a struggle near the haystack that stood next to the spot, were evidence that she seems to have resisted in a most determined manner.

The following morning as Mr Stubbs, the owner of the land, was going across the fields, the marks of the struggles struck his attention and he gave alarm. Footprints were traced to the neighbouring field where there was a pit, and there was discovered the body of the unfortunate woman in a most deplorable condition. Her mouth was stuffed with hay, her body was covered with only a silk handkerchief, and her hands were tied behind her. On her head and side were several marks of violence that would have been inflicted with a hay fork, which stood near the spot.

This was deemed sufficient evidence to convict the prisoner of her murder. The jury retired only for a few minutes and brought in their verdict of guilty. The judge then passed the sentence of the law upon the prisoner, that he should be executed on Saturday morning next, and that his body given to the surgeons for dissection. The sentence was duly carried out.

There is reason to believe that Johnson died penitent, as is evidenced by the following letter he sent to his wife:

> Dear Ellen, Shrewsbury March 20th 1822. If I may be allowed the expression, I write to you for the purpose of expressing my thankfulness to you since my confinement and I confess I am deserving of my fate. I would now fill up the few remaining minutes of my existence in the humble of earnest endeavours to deter any of you from coming to my sad end. Had I resisted the first unlawful desire I should have crushed the seed from which sprung the hideous monster, murder. Had I listened to the advice of my parents I might have lived respected and died happy and now instead of my ashes mingling with the dust of my family and friends, no grave is allowed for my resting place, and no happy tongue shall wish my spirit peace. I can say no more, the bell calls me to an external world. Believe me to be, dear wife, your affectionate husband. SJ.

J

JACKFIELD

The village of Jackfield, near Ironbridge, sits proudly within the World Heritage Site of the famous Ironbridge Gorge and Coalbrookdale, the scene of the start of the Industrial Revolution. With its host of museums and picturesque sights, including the world's very first iron bridge, Jackfield has more than its fair share of odd goings-on and tragedies.

~ *The Tuckies* ~

The curiously named Tuckies is a tiny hamlet on the edge of the village of Jackfield. Unfortunately it is prone to flooding, with Ferry Road being particularly vulnerable when the waters of the River Severn rise. The Boat Inn, on the western bank, displays water levels in its doorway. Opposite the pub is the Memorial Footbridge, opened in 1922, which links the Tuckies with Coalport on the eastern bank, near the famous Tar Tunnel, and the inclined plane, both part of the Ironbridge Gorge Museum. A little way south of the Tuckies is where the lost village of Werps once stood.

~ *The Tuckies Ferry Disaster* ~

Just after 9 p.m. on 23 October 1799, the Tuckies Ferry set off in the dark from Coalport to take workers at John Rose & Company Porcelain China Works across the River Severn to their homes in Jackfield and the surrounding area. But when the vessel reached mid-stream, the boat mysteriously sank without warning. On board were forty-one people, most of whom had just finished their shift at the China Works. Of these, only thirteen survived, and the other twenty-eight, of whom fifteen were women, drowned. In the darkness the cries for help rang out across the water, but friends and family on the bank were unable to provide any assistance. The reason for the disaster has never been forthcoming, for although the river at this point flows very rapidly, that night the flow was reported as being nothing unusual. The boat's crew were experienced in making the crossing, thus adding to the mystery.

Many of the bodies were recovered the next day, some a great distance downstream from the scene of the accident. A number of bodies remained underwater for a month before they too were able to be recovered; the bodies of a few unfortunate souls were never found.

The Tuckies Ferry, also known in the area as the Coalport Ferry or the Werps Ferry, had been opened by local industrialist and ironmaster William Reynolds (1758–1803), to provide workers with a better and more convenient access to their place of employment.

When the river level was low, the boat would be swung crossways and secured to each bank to form a bridge over which the workers could cross. The ferry operated for 120 years, before being made redundant by the building of the Memorial Footbridge.

The Boat Inn at Jackfield.

The Memorial Footbridge.

~ Man Overboard ~

Tragedy struck the Tuckies Ferry again 101 years later, when on 20 January 1900, 72-year-old John Harrison, who had been in charge of the ferryboat for more than twenty years, lost his balance and fell backwards into the river while lighting a lamp, and was swept downstream by the torrent of the swollen river. His fall was witnessed by two people: Jane Emily Brocksidge, a school teacher; and boatman Henry Wild. Mr Harrison's badly decomposed body was dragged out of the river forty-one days later at Bridgnorth, 10 miles downstream.

K

KETLEY

~ Murder Most Horrid ~

John Griffiths, a cooper by trade, lived in a house he had recently built in Ketley, where he carried on his trade, and near to the home of a 64-year-old collier by the name of William Bailey, a Methodist. Mr Bailey worked at the Old Park Iron Works, and the two neighbours were considered by many to be friends, Bailey having displayed many acts of kindness towards Griffiths. However, John Griffiths, aged about 28, was a bad-un, having been twice convicted of crimes. It was known that this former felon had frequently pestered William Bailey to loan him money, which Bailey had refused. On the morning of 1 February 1812, William Bailey's bloodied and battered body was discovered.

The previous day it had rained heavily, muddying the roads considerably, but Bailey's shoes were suspiciously clean, leading the investigators to believe that he had been murdered somewhere else and his body carried to where it was discovered. The search for evidence moved to Griffiths' new house, which was around 100 yards from where the body was found. Bloodstains were seen on a wall, and there was also a large amount of sand scattered on a spot on the floor. When the floorboards were taken up they were found to be stained with blood, and coagulated blood was found underneath. Subsequently a shirt, marked with William Bailey's initials, was discovered in the cellar, hidden under some coal. The damning evidence was a bloodied cooper's adze, corresponding in size to the indentations found on Bailey's head. A large horse pistol was discovered hidden behind some brickwork. None of Griffiths' dirty work clothes could be found, however, his wife had been washing the previous night.

A woman whose home was within 20 yards of Griffiths' told the investigating officers that at about 9 p.m. on the night of the murder she had seen Griffiths leave his house, check the street in both directions then step back inside his door, before reappearing pulling a large, heavy bag, which he dragged off in the direction of where Bailey's body had been found. A bag resembling the one the woman had described was found in Griffiths' house; it contained an amount of coagulated blood. It was also discovered that William Bailey's house had been robbed of anything of value.

Griffiths was arrested and subsequently found guilty by the Coroner's Court of the wilful murder of William Bailey on 31 January 1812; he was sent for trial at Shrewsbury Assizes, where the jury had no hesitation in finding him guilty as charged. Griffiths later made a full confession of his guilt and was hanged at Shrewsbury on 23 March 1812.

KINNERLEY

~ Dobbin and Golden ~

There is a curious story of a farmer from the Kinnerley area who one day sold two nice fat cows at the Shrewsbury 'Beas Fair' (cattle fair). Their quaint names were Dobbin and Golden. On his way home from the fair, the farmer passed by a furnace where the bells of the church of St Mary in Kinnerley were being recast. One of the workers asked the farmer what he would donate towards the cost, to which he replied, 'Dobbin and Golden'. He then took out his purse and proceeded to tip silver coins into the furnace.

Since that day the two bells have been known as Dobbin and Golden, in honour of the generous benefactor. These two bells cast with silver alloy in the metal emit a sound sweeter than the third bell (cast in 1732). One of the two bells bears the date of 1685, while the other is inscribed with the letters of the alphabet.

St Mary's church, Kinnerley.

KINLET

~ Message in a Bottle ~

Kinlet Hall is home to a special bottle which, until 1900, reputedly lay beneath the monument to Sir George Blount, who died aged 67 on 20 July 1581. The man was a colourful character who was known to possess a short fuse and to have been involved in a number of lawsuits during his lifetime. The bottle in question was allegedly used to fulfil a sinister function, for it contains the ghostly spirit of Sir George, who is said to have haunted the hall until some time in the 1700s. The bottle was reported as being 7 or 8in long, with a glass stopper in it which apparently nobody could remove.

Sir George inherited Kinlet Hall and its estates in 1531, following the death of his father, Sir John Blount. George was a staunch Catholic whose sister was the famous Elizabeth (Bessie) Blount, mistress of King Henry VIII. He was born during the reign of Henry VIII, and lived during a time of great religious upheaval in England following the king's break with Rome. He saw three other monarchs ascend to the throne: Edward VI, Mary I, and Elizabeth I. In 1570, he allegedly threw out his wife, Constance (*née* Talbot).

When his daughter Dorothy defied him, Sir George disinherited her in favour of his nephew, Roland Lacon, the son of his sister Agnes who had married Sir Richard Lacon of Willey. Dorothy tried to have the settlement reversed, but her appeal was unsuccessful. The story goes that he died in a rage because Dorothy had disobeyed him and had married a man reputed to be her pageboy.

Subsequent owners of the hall grew increasingly annoyed with Sir George's ghost, which kept appearing, riding his horse throughout the hall and across the banqueting table – a bit off-putting for guests during dinner parties. Their solution was to get a priest in, and for him to coax George's spirit into a bottle – the one under the monument.

So what of the bottle? Well, in 1900 a curious antiquarian decided to investigate the myth further and take a look at the notorious 'unopenable' bottle. He pulled the glass stopper and found that it contained ... not the ghostly spirit of Sir George, but a quantity of photographic developer!

~ King Henry's Bastard ~

A famous Shropshire connection with King Henry VIII is a woman by the name of Elizabeth Blount, sister of the aforementioned George Blount. Bessie Blount, as she was known during her lifetime, was born at Kinlet some time between 1498 and 1502, the daughter of Sir John Blount of Knightley and Kinlet, and Catherine, *née* Pershall. Little has been previously recorded of Bessie's early life, but we do know that she was blessed with a rare beauty, although sadly there is no known portrait of her in existence.

Her father, loyal servant of the king, had accompanied King Henry to France in 1513, during the war against the French king, Louis XII, holding the office of Captain of the Army that besieged Tournai. Seven years later he was witness to the peaceful royal meetings at the 'Field of the Cloth of Gold'.

The Blounts' manor at Kinlet was very near to the manor of Bewdley, where the young Prince Arthur, Prince of Wales (born 19 September 1486), had set up court, therefore it would seem unbelievable that Sir John and his family would not have visited the prince to pay their respects. Prince Arthur plighted his troth to Catherine of Aragon in her absence on 19 May 1499, in the chapel of the Manor of Bewdley.

On 27 September 1501, Catherine of Aragon, two months short of 16 years of age, arrived in England to fulfil a matrimonial contract with the 15-year-old Prince Arthur, brokered by her father, King Ferdinand II of Aragon, and the avaricious English King Henry VII, who wanted the generous marriage dowry that Catherine brought with her. The marriage took place on 14 November 1501, and the young couple set up court at Ludlow Castle. Bessie's grandfather, Sir Thomas Blount, was Steward of the Royal Park and Manor of Bewdley at that time, and so would have known the prince, and accordingly paid regular visits to his court. Unfortunately, on 2 April 1502, a little short of five months later, Prince Arthur died.

The king decided that the Spanish princess was too profitable a prize to lose and proposed a new match, between her and his second son, Henry (born 28 June 1491), who had been groomed for an ecclesiastical future. Catherine was almost six years older than Henry.

King Henry VII died on 21 April 1509, Henry VIII ascending to the throne on 22 April 1509, at not quite 18 years old. The couple were married on 11 June 1509, and Catherine was crowned queen on 24 June 1509.

There is no doubt that young Elizabeth Blount first travelled to court in Spring 1512, to become a maid-of-honour to Henry's new queen, Catherine of Aragon, where the young girl learned Latin and French. She became a competent performer on the virginal (a smaller keyboard instrument of the harpsichord family), and excelled in the arts of dancing and singing. Whilst at court Bessie was paid, in one year, the sum of 100 shillings, this is listed on a warrant (for his service in the same year, her father was paid £60 16*s* 8*d* as one of the king's spears).

As she grew into her teens, Bessie Blount was described by various dignitaries who met her as being eloquent and graceful, a blonde-haired beauty, noted for her flawless complexion and being an accomplished and most interesting person. After around two and a half years at court, Bessie was already attracting attention in the immediate circle of the king and his courtiers.

And of course it wasn't long before the young teenager caught Henry VIII's infamous roving eye. She became his mistress some time around 1514/1515, believed by many to be the first of his mistresses; Henry was around seven years Bessie's senior, if we take her birth as being in 1498.

Bessie remained the king's mistress for around eight years, unlike many of his other flings which usually did not last very long, although she was never afforded the title of *maitresse en tire*. Her union with the king was blessed with the birth of a son on 15 June 1519, whom they named Henry Fitzroy (Fitz or 'son of the', Roy 'or king', when using the old Norman method of naming a son), the only illegitimate child acknowledged by Henry VIII as his own. When he was older Henry Fitzroy had the titles of Duke of Richmond and Somerset, and Earl of Nottingham conferred upon him. Unfortunately this otherwise happy event appears to have changed the king's feelings somewhat, for it was not long after Fitzroy's birth that the king began an affair with the 'other Boleyn sister', Mary Boleyn. It was following this development that, in 1522, Bessie agreed to enter into an arranged marriage with Gilbert Tailboys, 1st Baron of Kyme, now almost completely disappearing from court and from official records. Bessie and Gilbert went on to have three children together.

New compelling evidence has come to light that suggests Bessie's daughter, Elizabeth (Tailboys), born around 1520, was most likely to have been fathered by the king. However, this child was never recognised by the king as being the fruit of his loins.

By 1529, when the king had taken a new mistress, Anne Boleyn, it was reported that a court chaplain passed a comment to the effect that Bessie was better looking than the king's fiancée, namely Anne Boleyn.

Bessie's husband Gilbert died in 1530, leaving her extremely well-off. She was pursued by a number of suitors including Leonard Gray, but finally chose to marry Edward Clinton, 9th Baron Clinton. Bessie died on 1 January 1540.

KNOCKIN

~ *A Strange Case of Love* ~

The small village of Knockin (pronounced 'Nukkin' by locals), is situated between Oswestry and Shrewsbury a little way north of Kinnerley. Its original motte and bailey castle was founded between 1154 and 1160 by Guy le Strange. The local shop is imaginatively called The Knockin Shop.

When Norman Knight Hamon le Strange (*c.* 1232–73), son of John le Strange III (1194-1269), of Knockin Castle set out to fight alongside Prince Edward of England in the first crusade, little did he know that he would meet the love of his life.

Prince Edward took the Crusader's Cross in an elaborate ceremony on 24 June 1268, sailing from Dover for France on 19 August 1268, together with 225 knights, including Hamon, or Hamo, or Haymo (Raymond) le Strange, who himself supplied a body of eleven knights, including his brother Robert le

The Knockin Shop.

Strange. This holy crusade was to be led by King Louis IX of France, but when Louis died unexpectedly, the crusade was postponed until spring 1269, however, it wasn't until 9 May 1271 that Edward finally landed at Acre in the Holy Land (around 22km north of the Israeli city of Haifa).

En route to the Holy Land, Hamon and the rest of the crusaders stopped off on the island of Cyprus where he met the beautiful 20-year-old Isabella of Ibelin (Isabeau d'Yberlin), the widowed Queen of Cyprus, and daughter of Jean d'Ibelin, Lord of Beirut, whom Hamon wooed and married in 1272. At a young age Isabella had been betrothed to Hugues II, boy King of Cyprus, and when he died aged 14 before the marriage was consummated, she ruled independently. Isabella was noted for her 'notorious lack of chastity'.

Sadly, theirs was a short marriage, because a year later Hamon died in the Holy Land in 1273. Mind you, Isabella continued to have men in her life. She returned to Beirut from Cyprus following the news of her husband's death, and not long after this she was taken back to Cyprus by Hugues III, King of Cyprus and Jerusalem, to be married.

She married twice more, firstly to Nicolas l'Alleman, Lord of Caesarea, and then to Guillaume Berlais. She had no children and died aged 30 in 1282.

~ *Who's That Knockin?* ~

Some time around the turn of the seventeenth century, a man by the name of Thomas Elks, of Knockin, committed a foul and calumnious crime: the fiendish uncle drowned his own nephew. In his *History of Myddle*, Richard Gough tells us all about this dastardly deed.

Following the death of his brother and his wife, Thomas Elks believed that it was he that should have inherited a fortune, however, his orphaned young nephew, who lived with his guardian grandmother (Thomas Elks' mother), had been named sole beneficiary. Elks' mother had indulged her son's extravagances until her own money had run out. Elks, convinced that the boy stood between him and being rich, hatched a plan to do away with the boy so that the fortune would come to him. He paid a poor boy to entice the nephew into a cornfield, ostensibly to pick wild flowers, where the evil Elks waited (the corn at that time was at its highest and so would mask the heinous crime he was about to commit).

When the two boys arrived in the field, Elks sent the poor boy home, then grabbed his struggling nephew, shoving the boy's head into a pail of water. Satisfied with his devilish work, he departed, leaving the drowned boy's body to the carrion and wild animals. That evening the alarm was raised that the boy was missing, and a search of the area was organised. Thomas Elks had made more than one mistake, because on hearing the news, the poor boy came forward, telling how Elks had hired him, and how the two boys had gone to the cornfield, and how he saw Elks take away the struggling nephew in his arms. A search of the cornfield revealed Elks' other mistake: the dead boy's body. Learning this, Elks took flight on the road to London, but he was seen by a neighbour who informed the authorities.

Two men were sent after the murderer, pursuing him almost to the capital. As the men rode along the road to Mimms in Hertfordshire, they spied two coal-black ravens in a field sitting on a stack of hay, tugging at the hay with their beaks and making hideous cries. Suspicious, they dismounted and went to investigate the cause of the ravens' behaviour. They found Thomas Elks asleep in the hay and apprehended him. Elks confessed that after he had killed the boy the two ravens had followed him everywhere he went. He had constantly sought refuge and hid, but wherever he went the ravens followed. Elks was brought back to Shropshire and was tried at Bridgnorth Assizes, where he was sentenced to death for the murder of his nephew. He was hanged on a gibbet on Knockin Heath.

L

LITTLE DAWLEY

~ The Springwell Pit Disaster ~

At around 4.30 p.m. on Friday, 6 December 1872, eight young men tragically lost their lives at the Springwell coal mine in Holly Lane, Little Dawley, when links in a raising/lowering chain snapped. The men had just finished a gruelling shift in the 450ft-deep pit. As they hooked themselves onto the chain that would hoist them to the surface, they must have been looking forward to washing off the dust and getting something to eat and drink. Tragically, when the men were about 150ft from the bottom of the pit shaft, one or more of the links of the chain snapped, plunging the men to their deaths. Seven of the eight were killed outright by the fall and by the weight of the 1-ton chain landing on top of them; the eighth man died of his injuries soon after he was brought to the surface.

The winding method used at this pit was done by a triple-linked chain to which was fastened a short length of chain, which in turn had eight loops of chain attached to it, and the men sat in the loops. The device was known as 'The Doubles'. At the end of the triple-linked chain, situated above the heads of the men, was a round wooden shield called a 'bonnet' to protect the group of eight men (called a bond) from falling objects. In those pre-health and safety days there were no safety helmets with lamps and hi-vis jackets; the men usually wore cloth caps, and carried candles.

The bodies of the eight men were taken to the Crown Inn in Little Dawley, and laid out for identification. Their names were: Isaiah Skelton, 14, of Little Dawley; Robert Smith, 18, of Holly Hedge; John Davies, 19, of Brandlee; Allen Wyke, 20, of the Finney; John Yale, 21, of Dawley; Edward Jones, 21, of the Stocking; William Bailey, 21, of the Finney; and John Parker, 22, of Holly Hedge. All were miners except John Davies, who worked as a filler. William Bailey was the only married man, and he left a wife and child.

A crowd estimated at over 10,000 people came to pay their respects at the funeral which took place at Holy Trinity church in Little Dawley, and at their ensuing burial in the churchyard there, known as the Springwell Pit Communal Grave.

The subsequent inquest into the the Springwell Pit Disaster at the Top Yard Colliery was told that earlier that week, men had commented on the poor condition of the triple-link chain, which consisted of three separate lengths of chain into which were inserted wooden wedges to prevent the chains from twisting. It was also reported that some of the worn rivets had been replaced, and that a spare/replacement chain that had been purchased by the company had not yet been fitted.

The coroner found that the breaking of a chain was the cause of the tragedy, but then went on to single out the Coalbrookdale Company's engineer, William Heighway, and the company's overall pit manager, Henry Rawson, for systematically neglecting their duties, although no charges were ever brought against the two men or indeed against the Coalbrookdale Company.

Life goes on, and the following day work at the mine resumed. It closed some time around 1880.

LLANYMYNECH

~ *Ogo's Hole* ~

The area around Llanymynech and the beautiful hill of that name is honeycombed with mineshafts and passages, possibly from as long ago as 200 BC. The Romans mined copper here, and there are also deposits of lead and zinc. One such shaft is Ogo's Hole (*Ogo* is Welsh for cave, *Ogof* is Welsh for a cavern), a disused copper mine set on a hillside. It is said by some to be the entrance to fairyland, a tale that has spawned many curious legends.

One version of the legend concerns a poor old blind fiddler who, one day, inadvertently wandered into Ogo's Hole and lost his way in the passages. Having entered, he never returned, but sometimes in the cellar of the local public house his fiddling can still be heard.

In another version of the story, the fiddler went by the name of Ned Pugh, who one day bragged that he could walk from Ogo's Hole to the Lion Inn in Llanymynech. No one believed that this was possible, but he was adamant and so a wager was made, and on the appointed Sunday he set off, entering the cavern. His music was heard subsequently, but he was never seen again. The tune he plays became romantically known as 'Farewell Ned Pugh'.

The pub in Llanymynech has a second distinction in that it straddles the English–Welsh border. Not so long ago when it was illegal to drink in Wales on a Sunday, local imbibers could only drink in the English half of the pub.

~ The Giant's Grave ~

There is a legend about a giant who, long ago in the mists of time, buried his dead wife on the Shropshire side of Llanymynech Hill. A mound that can be seen there is her grave, known as 'The Giant's Grave' (*Bedd-y-Cawr* in Welsh). The hill itself is crowned by a huge Iron Age fort and stands at the confluence of the rivers Vyrnwy and the Tanat. Unfortunately, the standing stones that once graced the spot have long since been destroyed by quarrying. An 1878 description of the site tells us that there were four standing stones capped with a large flat 7ft by 6ft slab, 18in thick.

Legend has it that the giant's wife was interred with a vast treasure, including a huge gold circlet which was placed around her neck. There are tales of many attempts to find the treasure, all of which have failed.

If you fancy yourself as an intrepid treasure seeker who is willing to take the chance of becoming hugely wealthy, then you should definitely give this a go. However, if you value your life you should approach this task with great care, as illustrated by the following tale.

It is a story concerning three brothers, who each sought to discover the gold circlet. In their haste and disregard for the solemness of the place, they violated the site, toppling the capstone that once crowned the stones, which they also pushed over. They never lived to find the treasure because they were all suddenly struck down dead by some unseen deadly force.

LONGDEN

~ The Last Drop ~

At 8 a.m. on Thursday, 9 April 1868, 35-year-old John Mapp (some reports put his age at 36) became the last person to be publicly hanged at Shrewsbury (the penultimate public hanging in England and Wales). The hangman was William Calcraft. Mapp had been tried before Sir Fitzroy Kelly at Shrewsbury Assizes on 23 March 1868. The jury had little trouble in reaching their verdict of guilty as charged, for the capital murder of 9-year-old (some reports put her age as 10) Catherine Lewis of Longden, near Shrewsbury.

Nine years earlier, in 1859, John Mapp had been transported, having been sentenced to ten years' penal servitude and transportation for the rape of a 60-year-old woman, but in 1866 he received a ticket-of-leave and returned to England. He was now employed as a farm labourer by farmer Mr Whitfield of Longden Wood, and lived with his parents in Summerhouse Lane.

The court was told that on Sunday, 22 December 1867, Catherine Lewis had spent the afternoon at the home of Ann Davies, leaving there to attend Sunday chapel on Longden Road. Before leaving, she asked Mrs Davies to pin a glass-and-brass brooch on her shawl. The service ended at 7.30 p.m., and Catherine headed for home along Long Lane, walking in company with Jane Richards and Mary Hartshom. John Mapp had also been at the service, and he joined the three girls. Mary left the others at Longden Common Crossroads and, shortly after, Jane said goodbye and set off for Whitfield Farm, leaving Catherine and Mapp to continue their journey home.

On the following morning, Monday, 23 December, 16-year-old John Aston was ploughing a field belonging to Mr Whitfield, adjacent to Long Lane. Also working in that field was John Mapp, who was spreading manure. At about 10 a.m. the two men stopped working to eat their lunch, sitting on the ground near a holly bush. John Aston found a black straw hat covered in bloodstains stuffed in the bush. Puzzled, he showed it to Mapp, who told him to bury it. He didn't. Instead he placed the hat by the entrance to the field. The hat was spotted by Mary Hartshom, who was passing by. She recognised the hat as belonging to Catherine Lewis. Mrs Lewis became considerably upset when Mary showed her the hat. Catherine had not returned home after chapel, but the family hadn't been worried as she sometimes stayed overnight at the Davies' home. Mr Lewis went off to search for his missing daughter. He found marks on the ground indicating that someone or something had been dragged along, and followed the marks to an old hovel. He found Catherine's lifeless body inside. Her throat had been cut and her brooch was missing.

When a patch of blood was discovered near the holly bush covered over with manure, suspicion fell on John Mapp. A search of his house revealed the missing brooch, hidden in the pocket of his coat. Bloodstains were found on his coat and trousers, which he insisted were from a nosebleed he had suffered. When a bloodstained knife was also found at his home, he was arrested.

Mapp continued to protest his innocence right up to the eve of his execution, when he made a full confession. These are his chilling words reported at the time:

> When I parted with Jane Richards at the Short Lane gate, Catherine Lewis and myself walked together for a few yards. I ketched hold of her hand, and she said, 'Do you live by Edward Mason's?' and I said 'Yes.' When I had her by the hand she began to cry, and I believe she shouted out, but I am not quite sure. She ran to the gate and got over it – I suppose she was frightened at me. As she got over it I was close after her, and when I got over it the gate fell, but I did not fall. When I got up to her she was lying under the hedge, and I asked her to let me do something to her. She said she wouldn't let me. She then told me she'd tell her father. She was crying. I said to her, 'Well if you tell your father I'll cut your throat.' I then pulled out my knife and I cut her throat. She was lying on the ground, and I was kneeling at her left side. I got up and wiped the knife with some grass, and then wiped it on her pinner.

> I then undid the shawl and put the brooch in my pocket, and then put the shawl in her mouth. I am not, however, quite certain whether I pushed the shawl into her mouth before I cut her throat or afterwards, but I did put it in. I then got up and turned her head round, and pulled her down the field by her right hand. She was not dead when I started with her, but she was quite dead before I got to the bottom of the field. I put her in the building where she was found I think the mark on her forehead was caused by the heel of my boot touching her as I pulled her down the field. I did not strike her. I was very sorry after I done it.

A huge crowd, estimated at around 5,000 people, turned out to witness Mapp's execution, which was carried out on the prison gatehouse roof. What they saw was an horrific spectacle. As Calcraft slipped the noose over the condemned man's head, Mapp turned so that the displaced noose now sat under his chin and when the drop came it was not a clean death. Mapp struggled hard for what must have seemed to him to be an age, but in fact it was less than a minute.

LUDLOW

The wonderful old market town of Ludlow, with its historic castle, buildings and quaint streets, has more than its fair share of curiosities.

~ *The World's First Female Computer* ~

Mary Edwards (1750–1815) was the first ever female computer. She lived and worked from her house at No. 4 Brand Lane, Ludlow, where a blue plaque has been put up to signify her outstanding contribution to the *Nautical Almanac*. She was employed by the Board of Longitude to compute astronomical tables for the *British Nautical Almanac* between 1773 and her death in 1815.

In the days before mechanical or electronic computers were invented, the job of computers and comparers was to take observational data and turn this into a standard form through a series of long and tedious calculations.

The *British Nautical Almanac* was published annually, first in 1766, giving the position of the heavenly bodies at stated points of time, enabling the accurate navigation of shipping.

Mary's association with the *Almanac* came about through her husband, John Edwards, who attended Shrewsbury School and graduated from Magdalene College, Cambridge in 1771. A few years later, John was ordained into the Church of England. He worked as curate in Shropshire before, in 1778, being appointed preacher of Ludlow, a post he held until his death in 1784. Whilst at Cambridge he came to know Edward Waring, a Lucian Professor of Mathematics, member of the

Mary Edwards' blue plaque on the wall of No. 4 Brand Lane, Ludlow.

Board of Longitude, and fellow old boy of Shrewsbury School, who introduced him to the Astronomer Royal, Nevil Maskelyne (1765–1811).

Prior to Nevil Maskelyne's appointment as Astronomer Royal in the 1760s, almost all of the calculations for the *Almanac* were made by the Astronomer Royal himself, or by his assistant, at the Royal Observatory at Greenwich – an enormous task considering the vast number of calculations that needed to be done and then independently checked, so much so that Maskelyne recognised that he needed to put a team of computers and comparers together to be employed on completing this specific task. These people were paid by the Board of Longitude, each being supervised by the Astronomer Royal.

What were the qualifications for a computer? Considerable literacy and numeracy, the ability to use mathematical and astronomical tables, attention to detail, and of course neatness. It was deemed not to be necessary for a computer to have any knowledge of astronomy. During Maskelyne's period of office, between five and nine computers were employed at any one time, and one of these was Mary Edwards. Computers worked from home, many living in London, but like Mary there were some who lived and worked in other regions of England.

Mary held the distinction of being the first female to be professionally employed in this work until three more ladies were employed, in 1890, by Maskelyne's successor, William Christie, his one-time assistant.

Ludlow Castle, with Dinham Bridge in the foreground.

~ Pull the Other One ~

In medieval times a fierce tug-of-war used to be held in Ludlow's fair town. Two teams representing two different wards of the town competed against each other, struggling to tug a 36-yard-long rope with a blue knob at one end and a red knob at the other. The origin of the contest is said to date back to the Wars of the Roses, when the Yorkist town was besieged by Lancastrian King Henry VI and his forces. One group of citizens who supported the king struggled against another group who supported Richard Plantagenet, Duke of York.

The contest began when the town mayor dangled a rope from an upper window of the market hall, which had to be reached by two men and a woman from each team, standing on each other's shoulders. After this, the serious work began in earnest, the reds trying to tug the rope into Mill Street, and thence dip it into the River Teme, while the blue team tried to tug the rope into the Bull Ring, and thence dip the rope into the River Corve. Every time one team scored a successful tug, the rope would be brought back to the Market Hall, and the contest would begin again. The game was over when one team scored twice running. Finally the rope would be sold by public auction and the money spent on beer. The event gave rise to so much fighting, and resulted in so many injuries among the crowd and competitors, that in 1851 it was supressed.

Ludlow's eighteenth-century Buttercross at the top of Broad Street.

~ *Miracle at Ludlow* ~

At 2 a.m. in the darkness of the early hours of Thursday, 6 September 1956, Liverpudlian lorry driver James Reynolds smashed his articulated lorry into the Onibury level-crossing gates on the A49, a little way north of Ludlow, blocking the Hereford–Shrewsbury railway 'up' line. He could not have imagined the resultant disaster that would follow.

A short time later the line blockage brought the 4.45 p.m. Penzance–Manchester overnight passenger express train, carrying 150 passengers, to a halt several hundred yards north of Ludlow railway station, at the Ludlow signal box, where it was held. The 250-yard-long train consisted of six passenger cars, three bogie vans, a guard's van at the rear, one bogie milk van, plus a brake second car, drawn by a 4-6-0 type tender engine, No. M45644.

At around 3 a.m., the guard, Mr J.E. Jones, descended from the train and made his way to the signal box to discover the reason why the train had been stopped. He then returned to the train and made his way along the corridors to the leading carriage, where he alighted and walked along to the front of the train to inform the driver the reason for the stoppage. This action saved his life.

The rear of the train was around 500 yards from the exit of Ludlow tunnel, and with all danger alerts having been activated there seemed no reason to be concerned. Unfortunately that was not the case, because steaming along at between 40 and 50mph on the same 'up' line was the 2 p.m. parcel train from Penzance–Crewe. This consisted of thirteen vehicles in total, drawn by an ex-GWR mixed traffic engine, No. W.9306, with a 2-6-0 wheel arrangement and a six-wheeled tender. The braking distance for the parcel train should have been around 364 yards, and with the danger signals in place the train should have had time to stop. Unfortunately it didn't. The engine of the parcel train ploughed into the back of the stationary express, pushing it 60 yards along the track. The wrecked train concertinaed into a melange of twisted metal and wood, as coaches splintered and were pushed on top of each other by the parcel locomotive.

In what can only be described as a miracle, every one of the 150 passengers aboard the express was able to walk away from the disaster, albeit suffering from shock to some extent. The driver of the parcel train hurt his leg and suffered from severe shock; he was unable to give evidence until 12 November 1956. The fireman and the guard on the parcel train escaped injury.

Within thirteen minutes the local Police and Fire Brigade were on the scene, with doctors and ambulances two minutes later. Breakdown cranes and crews from Shrewsbury and Cardiff arrived later to clear the wreckage. In the event,

The Feathers Hotel, Ludlow.

only the 'up' line was damaged, and the cleared line was able to reopen the following morning. The front portion of the express train was able to move forward at 6.25 a.m.

The inquiry by the Ministry of Transport and Civil Aviation, headed by Colonel W.P. Reed, concluded that somehow the driver and fireman of the parcel train failed to see the danger signals until it was too late to do anything to avoid the collision, and that the time of the incident – early morning – was probably the worst period of human consciousness and concentration.

That no one was seriously injured in this collision is surely a miracle.

M

MADELEY

~ The Swiss Vicar ~

Jean Guillaume de la Flechere, known locally as 'Fletch of Madeley', was born into a wealthy family in Nyon, near Lake Geneva in Switzerland. He came to England in 1750, arriving in Shropshire two years later to take up the position of tutor to the children of Thomas Hill at Tern Hall (which was demolished by the 1st Lord Berwick, Noel Hill, in 1783 to make way for his new mansion, Attingham Park).

In 1757, he was ordained in the Anglican Church, first as deacon and then as priest, becoming curate of Madeley. He was promoted to vicar of Madeley in 1760, staying there for twenty-five years.

During his time working as a tutor in London, he met and became a rare friend of the Methodist preacher John Wesley along with his brother Charles Wesley.

At the time of the start of Fletcher's ministry, Madeley was reputedly inhabited by the roughest of people, full of profanity and ignorance, who John Fletcher, as he was known, worked tirelessly to reform, facing many rebuffs and much violence. On Sundays he reputedly walked round the town at 5 a.m., ringing a handbell to wake up the people. This saintly man went without food to feed the poor, and taught local children in a day school as well as a Sunday school.

His tireless self-sacrifice took its toll on his health, but in 1770 a rich friend came to his aid and took him away to Italy and France for a period of recuperation.

John Fletcher died on 14 August 1785, and is buried alongside his wife in the graveyard at St Michael's in Madeley. John Wesley preached his funeral sermon, telling the congregation that he never met a man so holy, and adding that he never expected to do so on this side of Eternity.

St Michael's church in Madeley was rebuilt in 1796 by Thomas Telford, to the concept of John Wesley.

❖ MINSTERLEY ❖

~ *The Great Minsterley Flood* ~

Minsterley is normally a peaceful, quiet village in the Onny Valley, nestling at the foot of the Stiperstones, however, over the years that peace and quiet has been disrupted more than once.

On the afternoon of Monday, 27 May 1811, there was a terrific cloudburst above the Stiperstones. It was an intense storm so violent that from the tiny settlement of White Grit at the foot of Corndon Hill, on the border with Wales, reports came in of giant hailstones raining down from the blackened sky, some as big as 2in in circumference, pummelling the earth into submission until they lay almost 12in deep. Forked lightning blazed overhead, lighting up the sky. Local folk in Minsterley likened the sound of the rolling peals of thunder to a battery of huge cannons being fired.

The heavy rain created pools of water in seconds, but up on the nearby hills Mother Nature was brewing up much bigger trouble. A huge torrent of water sped down the hillside in the direction of Minsterley, building like a tsunami, splitting into different directions, one course taking an eastern route towards the village of Habberley. However, the main body of water swelled the valley through which ran the Minsterley Brook, which burst its banks in a split second. The raging torrent swept away everything in its path, including trees, vegetation and dwellings. One tree over 80ft high was torn up by its roots and floated away across open fields for over one mile, such was the sheer force of the water. Back at White Grit several miners' cottages were swept away, while the buildings at Hoxton Mills owned by Mr Nailor were completely devastated.

Between the hours of 5 and 6 p.m., the rampaging deluge struck Minsterley, flooding almost every house in the village. A local farmer was swept along on the wave for a distance of over 700 yards; he passed through the bridge, where the destructive torrent threw him into a pigsty, from where he somehow managed to climb up onto the roof of a nearby house. His sister suffered a similar fate, however, after being carried a long way, she found refuge in the branches of a tree. So battered and bruised was she that it was not thought she would survive. Another farmer's thrashing machine disappeared under the waves, and his stables disintegrated, but miraculously five of his horses managed to escape. Inside the Angel public house, thirteen customers believed they had managed to reach safety when on hearing the first alarm they dashed upstairs. Unfortunately, the ever deepening water chased after them, flooding the second storey of the building. The men managed to escape injury or worse by clinging to the rafters. The stable block plus all other adjacent buildings were swept away, but the seventeen horses got free and swam to safety.

Neither the monsoon-style rain nor the torrent of water was showing any sign of easing, and it now smashed into the stabling of the Reverend David Williams, curate of Holy Trinity church, carrying away that structure together with part of the church wall.

Three people of Minsterley perished in the tragedy: Mr Hoggins, a farmer; Mr Homes, a labourer; and one other person, not named. In some houses the water level was by now between 6 and 8ft deep. Further to the south-west of Minsteley, the mill and mill house at Plox Green were carried away.

The main torrent continued on its path of destruction, reaching the village of Pontesford, where the water smashed through windows, flooding the home of Mr Heighway to the extent that the walls of his house eventually gave way.

The west elevation of Holy Trinity church, Minsterley.

Mr Heighway's 83-year-old grandmother, together with two female servants and a labourer, were hurried to safety. Mr Heighway's wife plus another woman managed to escape the rising water by climbing onto the roof of the house. From there they espied Mr Heighway clinging desperately to a pole for dear life. Fortunately two men on the bridge around 30 yards away managed to haul him to safety.

An overseer at Pontesbury Coal Works, Mr Bennet, plus two others, took refuge in a hay loft, where they must have been praying to God for their safe deliverance when the barn building was swept away, killing all three men.

Mr Heighway later estimated that the cost of the clear up at his property would exceed £4,000, explaining that he had lost almost his entire house, all but the wing where his wife and her companion had taken refuge, together with all their furniture, stabling, barns, sheds, two valuable horses, tan-pits, hides, bark, and every fruit tree from the orchard. At this place the water was estimated to be at least 20ft deep.

North-east of Pontesbury at the Hanwood linen mills of Marshall, Atkinson & Company, the damage done by the torrent was considerable. The mill buildings, owned by Mr Blower and Mr Pickering, had sustained a great deal of destruction. Every bridge and mill within the course of the torrent was either destroyed or greatly damaged. At Cruckmeole, near Hanwood, two farmers reported that each of them had had at least one cow swept away.

The torrent continued unabated, following the course of the Meole Brook and reaching Coleham, a suburb of Shrewsbury, at about 10 p.m., accompanied by a tremendous roaring sound. The cellars and downstairs rooms of the Seven Stars public house, plus all the adjoining houses, were engulfed by the deluge. The street in front of Mr Hulbert's factory was flooded to a depth of almost 3ft. Shrewsbury is around 11 miles from Minsterley.

Eyewitness accounts described the noise of the current as being inconceivably dreadful, and said that the cries for help could be heard all around, contributing to the horror of the situation.

The force of this great body of water rushing into the River Severn from Meole Brook actually turned the normal current of the Severn, the level of which rose near the English Bridge by 4ft in height in less than ten minutes.

There was a great deal of damage done to the Abbey Watermill, and reports stated that the force of the torrent running under Coleham Bridge was so powerful that it carried with it several hundred square yards of an adjacent field. The death toll was high. Nine citizens of Pontesford lost their lives, plus three people in Minsterley.

The coroner at Bishop's Castle, Mr Wollaston, together with a jury, assembled to view the bodies that had been recovered, in order that the friends and families of the unfortunate individuals might pay their last respects.

The *Shropshire Chronicle* reported, 'No report such as this can hope to convey the degree of distress and calamity such as this tragic event has caused. Living in our inland situation we are not used to such scenes, the desolation to agriculture and property of every kind, the tragic loss of so many lives.'

It was estimated that in the parishes of Pontesbury, Worthen and Westbury, the floodwaters covered at least 3,000 acres of land, and a huge number of cottages had been destroyed. The *Chronicle* went on to say, 'Who shall tell the anguish of many a peasant, whose family is now perhaps homeless, and whose garden ground is laid desolate.'

An appeal was made and collections raised by the benevolent people of Shropshire soon reached £1,862.

The Rea Brook, like many other natural water courses, has always been subject to flooding. The earliest report of flooding in the area was in 1338, but it was the 1811 disaster, known as either the Minsterley Flood or the Hanwood Flood, that caused the most devastation, washing away houses, sheds, cattle, walls, trees and bridges.

Since then there have been other major floods in the area, in 2000, and again in 2007, the latter seeing another bridge washed away. The Rea Brook runs some 30km from Marton Pool (a site of special scientific interest) to join the River Severn at Shrewsbury, near the English Bridge.

~ *The Tragic Case of Dennis O'Neill* ~

A wartime tragedy concerned the sad case of young Dennis O'Neill. Dennis was 12 years old when he and his two younger brothers came under the care of Newport County Borough Council in South Wales, who decided that the three brothers were in need of care and attention, and so Newport Education Committee decided to relocate the boys – Dennis, 12; Terence (Terry), 9; and Frederick (Freddie), 7 – to Shropshire. Dennis and Terry were to live with childless Reginald Gough and his wife Esther at Bank Farm, near Minsterley, in return for £1 per week. Young Freddie was to be lodged in the home of Mr and Mrs Pickering. The Goughs had married in February 1942, after Esther had left the Women's Auxiliary Air Force in June 1941.

Early on the afternoon of 9 January 1945, Mrs Gough, aged 29, phoned for a doctor, reporting that Dennis was having a fit, and would the doctor come out to the farm to see him. When Dr Holloway Davies arrived at 3.30 p.m. he discovered that the boy was dead, in his opinion having died between four and six hours earlier. Dr Davies noticed that the boy was in an appalling condition, which he reported to the authorities.

At the subsequent inquest, the coroner found that Dennis had died of cardiac failure after being struck by several heavy blows to his chest. A close examination of the boy's body had revealed severe injuries to Dennis' back, believed to have been the result of being beaten with a heavy stick. Dennis was also found to have been undernourished to the extent that his frail body was thin and wasted, and well below the normal weight expected in a boy of his age. Additionally his feet were covered with septic ulcers, and his legs were severely chapped.

Reginald Gough was charged with manslaughter on 3 February 1945, and Esther Gough was charged with wilful ill-treatment, neglect and exposure likely to cause suffering and injury. She was later charged with manslaughter on 12 February. The pair were committed to appear before Pontesbury Magistrates' Court on 13 February 1945.

The court heard the testimony of Terry O'Neill, who described in graphic detail the ordeal that he and Dennis, but chiefly Dennis, had been subjected to. He explained that their daily ration of food was a meagre three slices of bread and butter, plus tea, but admitted that he and his brother supplemented this by stealing whatever they could filch from the kitchen pantry. Terry's heart-wrenching story included the fact that in desperation Dennis would even suck milk directly from the teats of cows, and that each night both boys received a thrashing on their hands and legs, sometimes each receiving up to 100 blows.

Terry testified that on 6 January, Dennis had been sent out to collect sticks, but when his brother returned with only a handful, Reg Gough beat him and forced the lad to stand in the freezing cold yard, where he stood shivering and crying until Esther Gough dragged him to the spinney by his hair. Starving, Dennis was caught biting into a swede and was again thrashed. Next day, Gough stripped Dennis naked and beat him so hard that the stick he was using broke. Not yet satisfied, Gough grabbed another stick and continued the beating until the boy's legs were blue and bleeding. The day after, Dennis was unable to stand, and when Terry returned from school he found his brother locked in a cubbyhole in the kitchen. Dennis' feet were in a terrible state and Gough beat him to stop him crying. Next morning when Dennis complained of pains in his back, Gough beat him with his fists. Poor Dennis O'Neill died that afternoon.

The following day during Terry's continued testimony, under cross-examination he admitted that he and his brother were sometimes naughty, and that they deserved to be punished. He also said that Gough had sometimes played football and cricket with them, and that they were encouraged to say their prayers each night before bed. During this session Terry admitted that he and his brother ate the same food as the Goughs.

A clerk with Newport Education Committee, Miss Eirlys Edwards, stated that on her visit on 20 December 1944 she found that Dennis was ill and frightened, and recommended the two boys' removal to a more sympathetic home, and Shropshire Education Committee were so informed.

Police Sergeant Macpherson told the court that, following the death of young Dennis, he had observed that the boys' bedroom was dirty and ill-furnished. He said that Mrs Gough had told him that Dennis had complained of pains in his feet from the moment he came to live with her and her husband, and that he was always late in getting up. She also told him that the boys had been fighting on the day before Dennis had died, and that this was the cause of the marks on his body. She claimed only to have hit the boys when they had been naughty; this was also the claim of her husband.

The verdict was to commit Mr and Mrs Gough for trial at Shrewsbury Assizes; no bail was allowed. The trial was subsequently transferred to Stafford Assizes, and began on 15 March 1945.

It took the jury a mere twenty minutes to deliver their verdict, and on 19 March 1945, Reginald Gough was convicted of manslaughter and received a sentence of six years. Esther Gough was found guilty of neglect and sentenced to six months in prison.

It was revealed later that Gough had a history of violence, and in 1942 had been convicted of assault on his wife, who had left him in July of that year, applying for a separation order on the grounds of persistent cruelty. She subsequently went back to live with him again.

This tragic case raised questions in Parliament, and resulted in a public inquiry that criticised both councils for lack of inspection, and their failure to recognise the danger in placing children in the hands of a convicted and violent man. However, just as so often happens today, no one person or authority was named as being responsible for the decisions that cost young Dennis O'Neill his life.

~ *The Virgin's Garland*~

In the eighteenth century, Holy Trinity church in Minsterley had a rather picturesque way of honouring a girl who died unmarried, particularly if she had been betrothed at the time of her death. The custom was to display a 'Virgin's Garland', sometimes called 'Virgin's Crown' or 'Crants' (the latter derives from the German word *Kranz*) on her coffin, and then after the burial hang the garland in the church as her permanent memorial.

The garland is a structure like a crown made up of two intersecting arches on a hoop base, the whole thing being about 12in high. The framework is sometimes covered with white linen, onto which is sewn pink paper roses and white paper lilies, or, in other examples, black and white ribbon rosettes. Ribbons hang down from it, and sometimes one or more pairs of white gloves, either real or made of paper, are added. The deceased girl's name and dates are usually indicated, either on small labels hanging from the garland, or by inscriptions on the bracket supporting it. As well as in Minsterley, virgin's garlands have also been the custom at Astley Abbots, Acton Burnell, Shrawardine, Hanwood, and at the chapel in Little Ness.

William Shakespeare wrote about a Virgin's Garland in *Hamlet*, Act V, Scene 1. The priest replying to Laertes' question, 'What ceremony else?':

Replica Virgin's Garlands displayed in a glass case inside Holy Trinity church, Minsterley.

Her obsequies have been as far enlarg'd
As we have warranty. Her death was doubtful;
And, but that great command o'ersways the order,
She should in ground unsanctified have lodg'd
Till the last trumpet. For charitable prayers,
Shards flints, and pebbles should be thrown on her.
Yet here she is allow'd her Virgins Crants.
Her maiden strewments, and the bringing home
Of bell and burial.

MONTFORD BRIDGE

~ A Bridge Too Far ~

The Montford Bridge, carrying the old Holyhead Road over the River Severn (once the A5, now the B4380), was built between 1790 and 1792 by world-renowned engineer Thomas Telford. Previous bridges at Montford have been the scene of a number of historical events.

It was here in 1283 that Dafydd ap Gruffydd, Prince of Gwynedd and last native Welsh Prince of Wales, was delivered to the English. His own countrymen had captured him in a cave – some say it was a bog near Bera Mountain – and surrendered him as a traitor. He was loaded with chains and taken to Shrewsbury. The event was so monumental that King Edward (Longshanks) travelled to the

The Old Toll House, Montford Bridge.

town, summoning the first Parliament in which representatives of the commons took part by legal authority. They sent the wretched captive to a terrible, gruesome death for high treason against the king.

Dafydd became the first prominent person of royal lineage in recorded history to be hanged, drawn and quartered. He was first tied to a horse's tail then dragged through the streets of Shrewsbury to the place of his execution. He was hanged by the neck, and cut down still alive, then he was disembowelled, his entrails burning before his eyes, before his head and limbs were cut off. The same fate awaited William Wallace a couple of decades later.

Another tale about the old bridge concerns one of Shropshire's legendary heroes, sixteenth-century outlaw Sir Humphrey Kynaston. The story goes that one day word came to the sheriff that Humphrey had been seen crossing Montford Bridge over the River Severn, at that time a stone and wood structure. Knowing that in time the outlaw would have to return across the bridge, and hoping to capture the bandit, the sheriff laid an ambush. Having had a number of sections of wooden planks removed from the surface of the bridge, making a gap so big that he and his men believed no horse would be capable of leaping over, the ambushers waited.

Later that day, as Humphrey Kynaston approached the bridge en route to his hideout, the sheriff's men rose up to apprehend him – but the lawmen had not taken into account Humphrey Kynaston's prowess as a horseman, or the power of the highwayman's coal-black steed, Beelzebub. Seeing the ambush, the outlaw spurred Beelzebub to a full gallop. The dynamic duo raced toward the bridge at breakneck speed and in one huge bound leaped the wide gap in the planking to the other side – and freedom – leaving the sheriff's men perplexed, and very disheartened. (See 'Nesscliffe' for more about Sir Humphrey.)

MUCH WENLOCK

The Wenlock Olympics, founded in 1861 by Dr William Penny Brookes, are the inspirational birthplace of the modern Olympic Games.

~ St Milburga ~

Shropshire's own royal saint, Milburga or Milborough, has two wells in the county dedicated to her. Here is the legend of how the wells got their name.

Way back in the Dark Ages, Merewald (Merewalh or Merwal), sub-king of the South Shropshire and Herefordshire peoples known as the West-Hecanas or Magonsaetas, and brother of King Wulfhere, the first Christian King of Mercia, and his wife Queen (later St) Ermenburga, had three holy daughters. Their names were Mildgyth (St Mildgytha); Mildthryth (St Mildred); and Milburga (St Milburga) – sometimes referred to as Faith, Hope, and Charity. A devout Christian, Merewald wanted to promote the new religion and so encouraged his daughters to spend their lives doing good work and to develop and establish religious houses.

The seventeenth-century Renold's House in Much Wenlock, reputed to be haunted.

Saxon Princess Milburga was educated at the Frankish Monastery of Chelles Abbey in Paris. She returned to England some time around 690 AD, and travelled from Kent to Shropshire to establish a community of nuns and monks around the holy site of St Owen's Well in Much Wenlock (Owen was a sixth-century Welsh saint who lived in Shropshire).

Milburga's grandfather was the pagan King Penda of Mercia, the slayer of King Oswald of Northumbria (St Oswald) at the Battle of Maserfield, near modern-day Oswestry, in around 642 AD.

Milburga died on 23 February 715 AD, having spent around thirty-seven years as prioress at Wenlock. She was buried in the priory and her venerated tomb attracted many who wished to make a pilgrimage to be healed by her saintly remains.

Unfortunately the priory was destroyed, and with it her tomb, in around 874 AD by a party of raiding Danes. It was refounded by Lady Leofric, better known as Lady Godiva, in the early eleventh century; Cluniac Monks from La Charite-Sur-Loire in France discovered her lost bones in 1101, and re-established it as a place of pilgrimage, particularly for lepers. The relics were described by Bishop Odo as glowing and smelling sweetly.

This St Milburga's Well is situated in Much Wenlock just off Barrow Street in St Milburga's Court.

St Milburga's Well, Much Wenlock.

St Milburga's day is 23 February, however, the good folk of Wenlock used to hold their own festival on 'Holy Thursday' (also known as Maundy Thursday, Covenant Thursday, Great and Holy Thursday, Sheer Thursday, and Thursday of the Mysteries), the Thursday before Easter, which commemorated the Last Supper of Jesus Christ.

The fun began after church service when the young men of the town, carrying green branches, paraded around the town on their way to St Milburga's Well, where they drank ale supposedly specially brewed from rainwater collected from Holy Trinity church. Women ate cakes and drank a concoction of sugar and water. Young maidens tossed 'crooked pins' into the well, at the same time wishing for a sweetheart. The fun continued with various traditional games with quaint names, and, for those not yet exhausted, a round of country dancing followed.

The second of the two wells is to be found at Stoke St Milborough (Godestock in the Domesday Book) at the foot of a steep bank leading to the Brown Clee Hill. The well water here is reputedly excellent for relieving soreness of the eyes, and was much used in days gone by for 'bucking' (a late medieval method of washing linen and clothes, still used in the nineteenth century).

~ *The Edge of Death* ~

On 13 April 1545, 11-year-old Alice Glaston of Little Wenlock was hanged at Much Wenlock along with two others, John Dodd of Little Wenlock, and William

Much Wenlock's sixteenth-century Guildhall, with the Corn Market (Buttermarket) underneath.

Harper, a tailor. Alice's burial is recorded in the parish register by Sir Thomas Botelar (Butler), a vicar and former Abbot of Wenlock. There is no record of Alice's crime, but she must surely be the youngest girl to be executed in England.
It is likely Alice was tried in the then recently built Guildhall at Wenlock, and taken from there to Edge Top for execution.

~ *The Turn of The Screw* ~

Victorian writer Henry James is reputed to have visited Much Wenlock on at least three separate occasions, in 1877, 1878, and again in 1882, staying at the Abbey, once the Abbot's house, which was the home of wealthy barrister and landowner Charles Miles Gaskell and his young wife Lady Catherine. At the time of his first visit, he was said to be working on his famous chiller *The Turn of the Screw*. James described the town and his stay in his travel essay *Portraits of Places*. A close friend of Charles Miles Gaskell, the American Henry Brooke Adams, facilitated James' stay in the town by introducing him to the Gaskells.

MYDDLE

~ *Myddle Historian* ~

At the beginning of the seventeenth century, a resident of the village of Myddle, Richard Gough, wrote two curious volumes, known locally as 'Gough's History of Myddle', in which he set down details of the lives and habits of his fellow citizens,

St Peter's church, Myddle.

entitled *Antiquities and Memories of the Parish of Myddle* and *Observations Concerning the Seates in Myddle and the Families to Which They Belong*. Packed with colourful anecdotes, criminals, family histories, and quirky facts, Gough's writings provide us with an invaluable insight into the lives of ordinary people in Stuart England.

Richard Gough was born in 1635, and was educated first at the village school in Myddle, and then at Broughton. In 1661, he inherited the family property at Newton on the Hill, and subsequently married Joan Peplow, with whom he had eight children (only four survived to adulthood). He was a yeoman, but was referred to locally as a gentleman. When he was around 28 years old, he became a churchwarden. In 1700, aged 66 and now a widower living with two of his daughters, he suddenly began writing about the people living in the village. The two volumes were produced over a period of two years. Readers of his work have commented on the detail of his memory and his acute powers of observation; perhaps he made notes throughout his life, however, there is no proof of this.

He began by setting down a plan of the church and the people who worshipped there on a pew-by-pew basis, describing each person's characteristics and foibles, including himself and his family, telling stories, some happy, some sad, and some downright scandalous.

One tale tells of three naughty girls who made a plot to poison their husbands – men who were addicted to gambling and alcohol. Only one succeeded and she took fright and ran away, but was 'arrested upon holiday, dancing on top of a hill in a company of young people'. He tells us of his own Aunt Katherine who 'was so extremely fat that she could not go straight through some of the inward doors of the house', and of a preacher who 'always wore, even while preaching, a dagger at his girdle', as well as the rector who was 'naturally addicted to passion'.

Gough wrote emotionally of his dear wife, who had 'died at Shrewsbury where she had gone to take physic', that she was 'too good to live with me and I not good enough with her to lie'.

Published twice, privately in 1834, and again in 1875, Richard Gough's work provides a fascinating account of life in seventeenth-century England.

Richard Gough lived through a turbulent period of English history – the English Civil War and through the dreary years of Oliver Cromwell's Commonwealth – and died in 1723. His manuscripts are lodged at the County Archives Office.

N

NEEN SOLLARS

~ The Disappearing Happy Wanderer ~

Three miles from Cleobury Mortimer lies the village of Neen Sollars, once known as Neen Baldwin. Its sister parish of Milton lies nearby. It was here, in the early seventeenth century, that the lord of the manor, Humphrey Conyngesby, was born around 1567. He grew up to be a great scholar and was famed as a traveller. In 1594, when he was 27, he embarked on a trek that would last four years and would take him to France, Germany, Italy and Sicily, before returning home. After only a short time in England the wanderlust got the better of him and he returned to the Continent, embarking on another adventure. This trip took him to Bohemia, Poland and Hungary, where he joined the forces of Rodulphe the Second, Emperor of the Romanes, as a voluntary gentleman, seeing service at the siege of Strigonium in Hungary against the Turks.

Following this escapade, Humphrey travelled to Turkey, and then to Anatolia, visiting Setos, Abydos and Troy, before hopping around the Greek Archipelago to Zant, Chios, Rhodes, Candy and Cyprus, visiting famous cities such as Arcadia, Corinth, Thessalonika, Ephesus and Athens, and thence to Constantinople, where he was honoured by Mohamet, third Emperor of Turkey, receiving many gifts. He stayed in Turkey just over a year before once again coming home, however, he was soon off again, this time to Spain. A quick trip back to England was followed by a new adventure, and he left London for Venice in October 1610. This trip proved to be his last, for Humphrey Conyngesby simply disappeared from the face of the earth, and was never heard of again. No one knows his fate.

In the south transept of All Saints' church in Neen Sollars, Humphrey Conyngesby's rather grand monument, erected to his memory in 1624, contains his reclining figure – a wonderful alabaster effigy depicting him, one elbow extended, his head resting in his hand as if in contemplation – and is inscribed with a detailed description of his travels.

Humphrey's journeys saw him away from England for a total of sixteen-and-a-half years in total. He never married; perhaps he never found the time.

NESSCLIFFE

~ *The Devil's Horse* ~

Nesscliffe is a rocky sandstone outcrop on the road between Shrewsbury and Oswestry, legendary for being the base of the infamous highwayman Sir Humphrey Kynaston – Shropshire's very own version of Robin Hood. Humphrey has also been likened to other legendary folk heroes such as Rob Roy and Dick Turpin.

Although his actual birth date is not known, some believe it to be in around 1474; we do know that Humphrey died in 1534. This youngest son of the High Sheriff of Shropshire, Sir Roger Kynaston and Lady Elizabeth Grey, Humphrey is sometimes referred to as Wild Humphrey Kynaston. He grew up in Myddle Castle, where the reckless and irresponsible young man was often in trouble, earning the nickname 'Wild' because of his madcap lifestyle.

At the Stretton Assizes on 20 December 1491, following one of his escapades, Humphrey, together with his brother Thomas Kynaston, and Robert Hopton, was convicted of the wilful murder of John Hughes of Stretton, and was subsequently outlawed by order of King Henry VII. To escape punishment, Humphrey lived in a cave in the sandstone cliff on Nesscliffe Hill (Kynaston's cave). From there, mounted on his famous horse Beelzebub, he embarked on a life of robbery, galloping down at top speed to relieve fat merchants of their cash and earning a reputation for robbing the rich and giving to the poor, a riotous and dissolute spree that lasted until around 1518.

The entrance to Nesscliffe Rock Cave is around 6m up the face of the cliff, once accessed via a weather-eroded staircase cut into the rock – until passage became

Sir Humphrey Kynaston's cave, Nesscliffe.

too dangerous. The cave has two chambers of about 4sq.m, one for Humphrey and the other for Beelzebub. Legend has it that the entrance once had an iron door, which later was used as the door to Shrewsbury Gaol. Carved into the sandstone wall are the initials 'H.K.' together with the date 1564 (obviously not made by Humphrey as he was dead by then).

In 1495, he inherited Myddle Castle from his father, but allowed the estate to fall into disrepair, and in the years following, Humphrey's many debts rose to unmanageable proportions.

Humphrey was married at least twice, firstly to Mariona ferch Williamus ap Griffith ap Robin (also named as Isabella Griffith, the daughter of a local farmer), and secondly to Isabella verch Meredith ap Howell ap Morrice de Oswaldestre, fathering at least eight children, possibly more if he married a third time, as another legend claims. It is claimed that Humphrey regularly patronised the Old Three Pigeons pub at Nesscliffe, and the seat he used can still be viewed, carved into the inglenook fireplace. The tavern is home to another tall story about Humphrey, who one day wandered in to get a drink and, seeing someone in his regular seat, took out his pistol and shot the man dead. There is talk of his ghost haunting the place.

Humphrey appears to have been well loved by the local people, who fed him and his horse – going out of their way to see that he wasn't captured.

Some believe that in 1493 he received a pardon from the king. Other accounts state that in 1513 Humphrey raised a force of 100 men to fight for King Henry

The Old Three Pigeons pub, Nesscliffe.

VIII, for which he received a royal pardon. Whatever the truth, we know that he died in 1534: his will is dated 1 May 1534, although the exact manner and place of his death remains a mystery. Some believe he died at a house in Welshpool. There is a far more romantic story suggesting that after succumbing to a fatal illness, he retired to his cave where a beautiful woman, famed for her skill, attended him, attempting to cure him of his malady. The woman turned out to be Isabella, his first wife. Her love for him had endured despite the years and ill treatment, and he died in her loving arms.

NEWPORT

~ *A Colourful Man* ~

Ten miles from Telford lies the picturesque town of Newport. A native of the town was the seventeenth-century irreverent satirist, poet and lampoonist Thomas Brown (1662–1704), of whom Sir Oliver Lodge famously composed the rhyme:

> Every merry wag throughout the town,
> will toast the memory of Brown,
> who laughed a race of rascals down.

Sir Oliver Joseph Lodge, physicist and inventor, was born in Penkhill, Staffordshire, and was educated in Newport. Lodge took up science, and sent telegrams long before Marconi.

The actual place of Thomas Brown's birth is thought to be either Newport or Shifnal, but for the purpose of the piece I have included him in the section on Newport, where he was christened in 1663. His father, William, was a farmer and tanner who died when young Tom was just 8 years old. He was educated on a free scholarship at Newport's Adams Grammar School, going on to Christ Church, Oxford University. His tutor there was the noted disciplinarian Dr Fell, of whom Brown wrote the anecdote:

> I do not love thee, Dr Fell,
> The reason why I cannot tell,
> But this know, and know full well,
> I do not love thee, Dr Fell.

Brown left Oxford without a degree, and became a schoolmaster, supplementing his income from his writing and translation services, making several enemies along the way with his coarse and scurrilous humour which contained profane and indecent pieces.

Thomas Brown died in 1704 and was buried in the grounds of Westminster Abbey.

~ *What the Dickens* ~

Charles Dickens' connection to Newport is that he reputedly based the character of Miss Havisham in his novel *Great Expectations*, published in 1861, on local Newport recluse Elizabeth Parker who lived at Chetwynd House. Dickens was a frequent visitor to Shropshire, particularly to Shrewsbury, and in his early years to Tong, where his maternal grandmother worked as housekeeper at Tong Castle. Whilst at Newport he stayed at the Bear Hotel, in Lower Bar (now Beaumaris House). Other reports suggest he also stayed at the appropriately named Havisham Court.

NORTON-IN-HALES

~ *'E's 'Armless, Yer Honour* ~

A curious tale from nineteenth-century Norton-in-Hales tells us that there lived a man who had no arms from the elbow down, whose name was Hugh Owen. He was a poor man who struggled against his disability to support his wife, Mary, and their four children. One thing he did own was an ass which one of his neighbours allowed him to graze on a piece of stubble land free of charge.

One day Hugh, accompanied by his little terrier, went to get the ass, and as they crossed a field a hare broke cover and took off at speed; naturally, the terrier chased after it. The dog caught the hare and killed it. Hugh was first on the scene but with no hands he was unable to pick up the dead animal. Minutes later, a local poacher came along and attempted to grab the hare, but somehow Hugh managed to send the poacher packing. Fortunately, next to appear on the scene was Hugh's 11-year-old son, sent by his mother to look for her husband. The boy retrieved the little dog's kill and carried it home for his mother to cook for supper.

Unfortunately this story has an unhappy ending because a nosey neighbour saw Hugh and his son with the hare and reported them to the authorities. Hugh was subsequently arrested and accused of poaching. He was brought up before landowner Sir Andrew Corbet, the local magistrate, who unsympathetically found Hugh guilty, sentencing him to pay the astronomically large sum of £20. As Hugh was unable to pay the fine, the heartless Corbet sentenced him to six months in prison.

O

OAKENGATES

~ A Load of Bull ~

Inhabited by tough colliers, the town of Oakengates can lay claim to the unenviable distinction of having been the scene of the last bull-baiting in Shropshire in 1833. The event was reported as being greatly attended by folks from far and wide, anxious to see the brutal contest (the previous year's meeting had to be cancelled due to an outbreak of cholera in the area). On this occasion the bull broke free from the stake and rushed madly among the crowd. There is no record of what happened next, only the comment that before the bull got free and, in the interests of fair play, only one dog was allowed to be let loose on the bull at a time.

OLDBURY

~ Panpudding ~

These days Oldbury is part of Bridgnorth, but in earlier times it was a separate settlement with its own parish church. Standing proudly between Oldbury and Bridgnorth, a little way behind Bridgnorth's Seven Valley railway station, is a roughly oval-shaped, steep-sided, flat-topped hill curiously known as Panpudding Hill. The mound is believed to have once been the site of a motte and bailey castle. Around 84m by 68m in base area, the summit is around 50m in diameter. The name of the promontory is said to describe its topographical shape – pan puddings were a sort of Yorkshire pudding, made of flour and eggs and cooked in a round pan. There are many instances where the name of this hill has been corrupted to Pampudding Hill, which no doubt derives from some ancient map where the name was incorrectly written.

Aethelflede, daughter of King Alfred and wife of King Aethelred of Mercia, built a fortification on the hill, probably of earth and timber, sometime around 912 AD, when she was busy constructing such strongholds across the line known as Danelaw: the border between land controlled by the Danes to the north and the Saxons to the south.

In subsequent centuries Panpudding Hill has played a significant role in various sieges: utilised by King Henry I in 1102, as a bailey in the assault on Bridgnorth

Bridgnorth railway station, which sits on the side of Panpudding Hill.

Bridgnorth Castle's Norman keep, leaning at an angle of 15 degrees, four times greater than the Leaning Tower of Pisa.

Castle held by Robert de Bellesme who was in open revolt against the king; in 1158, during the struggle for the throne of England between Stephen and Matilda; then again in 1321, during the Barons' Revolt; and finally in 1646, during the First English Civil War when, following a siege lasting twenty-six days, the castle was slighted by Parliamentary forces. Reputedly Cromwell's forces raised the height of the hill to increase the effectiveness of their cannons, which his troops had sited on the hill.

OSWESTRY

~ *The Wishing Head* ~

Oswestry is a town named after St Oswald, King of Northumbria, who was killed at the Battle of Maserfield, where there is a holy well dedicated to him. The battle took place near Oswestry on 5 August 642 AD (some put the year as 641), between two Anglo-Saxon kings.

Oswald, King of Northumbria, was a Christian, but was defeated by the pagan King Penda of Mercia and his Welsh ally, Cynddylan ap Cyndrwyn, King of Powys. After the battle, the victor, Penda, ordered a sacrifice to the pagan God Woden, and the head and limbs of his dead opponent were thus severed from Oswald's body and hung on trees and stakes. Legend has it that a swooping eagle snatched one arm and dropped it at Cae Nef (Heaven Field), where a spring miraculously burst forth from the ground – that place is now known as St Oswald's Well.

The name Oswald later morphed into Oswestry, from Oswald's Tree (in Welsh it's *Oswallt*, meaning Oswald's Cross). Oswald was subsequently venerated as a martyr and saint.

In company with most holy wells, St Oswald's Well has a web of elaborate rituals surrounding its use. Here's what you have to do: first you have to go there at midnight, then you must scoop up some of the water in one hand and drink some of it, while at the same time silently wishing for what it is you want; then you must fling the remaining water from your palm precisely against one particular stone in the wall forming the back of the well, and you will be granted your wish. The particular stone was originally a carving of St Oswald's head, but over time it has been worn down. It was originally believed that behind this stone was the actual head of St Oswald.

Another ritual doesn't specify the best time to go there, however, it does tell us that what you have to do is to place your lips close to the hole that resides in the stone archway of the wall and whisper your wish, then if you are lucky – hey presto!

And here's another bunch of rituals for you to try: make your wish whilst at the same time bathing your face in the cool, clear water; or try dropping a decent-sized stone into the water so that you make a splash that sends water onto your head, not

Eagle sculpture dedicated to the Christian King Oswald of Northumbria, Oswald's Well Lane, Oswestry.

St Oswald's Well, Oswald's Well Lane, Oswestry.

forgetting of course to make your wish; or – this one's a little more complicated – search around under the nearby beech tree until you find an empty husk that has markings on it that look like a face, then drop the husk into the water, making sure that the face floats upwards, and only if the husk stays afloat while you count to twenty will your wish be granted.

Imagine if everyone in Oswestry went along at midnight to test out the validity of these rituals – the place would be worse than Piccadilly Circus at rush hour.

P

PONTESBURY

~ *The Golden Arrow* ~

This story has nothing to do with the famous steam train of the same name, but it is rather fascinating. It concerns a legend that inspired the renowned Shropshire author, Mary Webb, to write her most famous novel, *The Golden Arrow*. She lived at Pontesbury, later moving to Lyth Hill.

The legend of 'Seeking the Golden Arrow on Ponsert Hill' is about an age-old custom that was popular up to the mid-nineteenth century, and is based upon the fanciful notion that a king, or some great person, once lost a golden arrow here.

The hill has been described as 'a grand isolated height', which some say is crowned with a likeness to that of a crouching lion; others say that it resembles the form of a coiled sleeping dragon. The twin summits rise out of the plains 8 miles to the south-west of Shrewsbury, and burst out of the earth some 650 million years ago. The summit divides into two: Pontesford Hill and Earl's Hill; both were once crowned with an ancient British hill fort dating from around 600 BC.

Back to the legend and the custom: on Palm Sunday, crowds of people would climb Pontesford Hill to look for the lost Golden Arrow. While they were searching they were entertained with wakes, involving much merry making, games of all kinds, and of course a lot of drinking.

There is an ancient, supposedly haunted, yew tree that sits on the hill, the only one of its kind that grows there. Legend states that the first person to gather a palm or sprig from the tree would come to no misfortune throughout the coming year, no matter what they might do or wherever they might go, providing they kept the palm safe. The sprig represents the palm branches carried at Christ's entrance into Jerusalem.

The next event in this fun-filled affair involved a madcap dash from the top of the hill in a hell-for-leather race to the Lyde Hole – a deep circular pool, fed by a tiny brook that winds down the hill to fall into a basin-shaped hollow. Locals once swore that this pool had no bottom. The winner of this competition was the first person to scramble down the steep sides of the hollow and then dip the fourth finger of their right hand into the water. That lucky person would then be certain to marry the first person of the opposite sex whom he or she happened to meet. Choosing was not an option, for the first you saw must be your fate.

Returning again to the legend of the Golden Arrow; if this valuable item is found it is predicted that some great estate will change hands, for it will never be found until the right heir comes along.

In the early 1870s, the elderly postmaster of nearby Minsterley declared that in days gone by a good fairy had ordained the search for the Golden Arrow, and had agreed to a condition: that she would undo some unknown curse, or spell, inflicted by a fiend or demon. But to be successful, the quest must be undertaken at midnight on Palm Sunday by a young maiden under the age of 20 (some say 21) and she must be the seventh daughter of a seventh son.

In the year 661 AD, Cenwalh, King of Wessex (648-674), and Wulfhere, King of Mercia (658-675), son of Penda, fought a great battle at Ponsentesbyrig, and there are some who believe that this was when the arrow was lost by one of the protagonists. Cenwalh was married to Penda's sister.

A quick word of cautionary advice needs to be added at this point: anyone climbing on the east crags must watch their step for if they descend the paths at dusk they might encounter the 'Pontesbury Archers', a mythical race of little men, known only to the locals, who lie in wait to shoot arrows at unsuspecting walkers.

PREES HEATH

~ *The Process of Scrying* ~

One dark night in September 1831, two barley ricks on a farm at Prees Heath went up in smoke. The fire raged out of control, setting fire to outbuildings, which were completely destroyed along with their contents, as were the two ricks of barley. The blaze spread to a cowshed attached to the end of the thatched farmhouse, in turn setting both on fire. The alarm was raised in the early hours of 13 September, and fire engines were sent for from Whitchurch.

The farmhouse was preserved by the swift action of two female servants who worked for Mr Kennerley of Heath Cottage, and by a boy, who brought a small engine from Mr Kennerley's, managing to keep the fire under some degree of control until the Whitchurch engines arrived. Aside from losing a large quantity of grain, Mr Nunnerly, the farmer in question, also lost five cows, two horses and ten pigs in the blaze, which also injured another cow and two pigs.

This fire followed a series of other fires in the area. The story goes that the farmer, John Nunnerly, was so puzzled by this mysterious occurrence that he was determined to find out more. He had heard that a certain 'cunning man', whose name was reputed to be Thorne, was an expert in the process of 'scrying'. Thorne resided in Whitchurch, and so Mr Nunnerly took himself off there to see this famous man.

Scrying, also called 'seeing' or 'peeping', is the age-old practice of inducing oneself into a semi-hypnotic or trance state, and gazing into a translucent object such as a crystal ball, in the sure and certain belief that things will be seen. Scrying is traditionally used for fortune telling, spiritual, and divination purposes.

Anyway, back to our story. Mr Thorne first required the farmer to swear an oath that his name would not be mentioned if the law became involved, and of course the farmer agreed, and so swore. Thorne then concentrated his powers, raising a vision of the farmer's yard, with the hay stacks still intact. Two men were seen moving stealthily around the yard, and then a spark of light appeared, glowing bright in the darkness. Thorne asked the farmer if he knew the names of the two men. The farmer replied that he knew enough, and with that returned to his farm.

The next day Farmer Nunnerly took out a summons against two young men, 32-year-old James Lea and 20-year-old Joseph Grindley, who lodged at the house of Mr George Whitfield in Heath Lane, not far from his farm. Nunnerly allegedly swore that he had actually seen them start the blaze that destroyed his barley ricks, his livestock and almost his house.

James Lea was arrested immediately, but Joseph Grindley had done a runner. However, he was arrested soon after in Burslem in Staffordshire, on, appropriately in the case of arson, 5 November. Both men were indicted for feloniously and maliciously setting fire to two stacks of barley, the property of Mr John Nunnerly, farmer, of Prees Heath in the parish of Whitchurch. The accused pleaded not guilty. Both later made statements putting the blame on the other.

The two men were found guilty and sentenced to be hanged, and both were said to have confessed their guilt on the scaffold. The executions took place in front of Shrewsbury Prison on Saturday, 31 March 1832, probably by the Chester hangman, Samuel Burrows.

Q

QUATFORD

~ The Church Built on the Promise of Love ~

Quatford is the scene of a romantic legend that is worthy of a mention. It concerns a Norman lord, Roger de Montgomery, loyal follower and cousin of William the Conqueror, who was granted lands throughout Shropshire for his service to the Norman invasion following the Battle of Hastings. He was the builder of many castles and places of worship, including a motte and bailey castle at Quatford, where there was an ancient river crossing. Roger's involvement in the battle is the source of some query. We know he supplied sixty ships to the invasion, but he either stayed behind in Normandy to help William's duchess, Matilda, rule the dukedom, or he commanded the Norman right flank in the battle.

Roger's first wife, who was known as the Wicked Mabel, was a cunning and treacherous woman who had earned a reputation for savagery. She was murdered in 1077, after taking a bath. Roger married a second time, this time to the excellent, amiable and virtuous Adelais (sometimes written as 'Adelisa' or 'Adelaid') de Breteuil (du Puiset), in Poitou, around 1080.

The story goes that some time after the Battle of Hastings, Roger travelled to England, then sent for his lady, Countess Adelais. She experienced a perilous journey from Normandy across the Channel, her first passage across that body of water. A great storm had sprang up, so fierce a raging tempest that the mariners expected nothing but shipwreck. Her chaplain fell asleep, and saw in a dream a comely matron who said to him:

> If your lady would be preserved from the danger of this dreadful tempest, let her vow to God that she will build a church to the honour of St Mary Magdalen in the place where she shall meet the Earl, her husband, in England, and specially where an hollow oak groweth near a hog-stye.

When the chaplain awoke, he recounted his dream to Countess Adelais, who vowed to build a church in accordance with the priest's dream, and suddenly the storm ceased.

The church built on the promise of love, Quatford, dedicated to St Mary Magdelene.

Adelais met Roger at Quatford in a wood where he was hunting, under a hollow oak as described in the dream (there is no mention of a pigsty). After hearing the tale and of his wife's vow, Earl Roger agreed to its fulfilment, and the church, dedicated to St Mary Magdalen, was built in 1086, on the prescribed spot on a hill adjacent to Roger's castle – it is known as the church built on the promise of love. The church is built of sandstone and tufa (a porous rock composed of calcium carbonate).

A short time before his death, Earl Roger became a monk at Shrewsbury, where he then spent three days in prayer and pious conversation, before dying on 27 July 1093/94. He was buried at Shrewsbury Abbey.

R

RATLINGHOPE

~ The Sin Eater ~

The rather odd custom of sin eating, sometimes known as the Funeral Dole, not only continued to be practiced in Shropshire, but also in many parts of the England/Wales border country, and in North Wales, Herefordshire and Breconshire. It involved the sin eater – usually a poor person, who was employed by the family of a person who had died suddenly without confessing their sins – to take away their mortal sins by eating bread and drinking ale over the body of the dead person. The corpse would be taken from the house and laid out on a wooden bier, then a loaf of bread was brought out along with a mazer (a hardwood drinking bowl) of ale (sometimes milk), which the poor person would consume over the corpse, thus eating the deceased's sins.

Shropshire novelist Mary Webb included the practice in her writings. The ritual was frowned upon by the Church, but the clergy generally turned a blind eye to the practice. Sin eating, with its pagan overtones, was widespread in the Middle Ages in various forms. Derivations of this can also be found in many areas of Europe and even in eighteenth-century America. Special cakes or bread were distributed to pall-bearers or mourners, known variously as corpse cakes, funeral biscuits, dead cakes and burial cakes.

The custom demanded that the dead met their maker clean of sin and in a pure state. Fear of the spirit of unshriven dead people, who had not recanted their sins, returning to roam the earth was also a contributor to the desire to rid the deceased of their sins – a form of apotropaic magic intended to ward off evil.

Often the sin eater would be a poor man or woman, sometimes a beggar, who most often was shunned by local society until they had need of their services. These sin eaters swallowed the free food and drink with relish, while the mourners swallowed the cost, for it was the custom to pay one groat, later one sixpence, to the sin eater. The sin eater's speech would include the following sentence, 'I give easement and rest now to thee, dear man or woman, come not down the lanes or in our meadows. And for thy peace I pawn my soul. Amen'.

The last recorded sin eater in Shropshire, and possibly England, would appear to be a man by the name of Richard Munslow, a well-known local farmer (not a poor man), who died in 1906 and is buried in the graveyard of St Margaret's church, Rattlinghope. The story goes that after three of his children tragically died in a whooping cough epidemic, Munslow took the decision to become a sin eater. In 2010, local people rallied round to raise around £1,000 to restore the monument marking Richard Munslow's grave.

The Sin-Eater Festival is now held every June at The Bridges, Rattlinghope. The festival is a combination of folk music, art, crafts, film and ale (sin-eater pale ale), where a giant wooden statue (a kind of wicker man) is burned.

S

SHIFNAL

~ Take a Sniff of This and See What Happens ~

This is the tale of the noted scientist and physician Thomas Beddoes, who was born in Shifnal on 13 April 1760. He was educated first at Bridgnorth Grammar School, and subsequently at Pembroke College, Oxford. He studied languages and science, earning his degree as Doctor of Medicine in 1786. He also studied medicine, chemistry and natural history in Edinburgh, and later, medicine in London. In 1788, he was appointed Professor of Chemistry at Oxford University, a post he left in 1792. Beddoes married Anna Edgeworth in 1794.

Armed with £1,000, bankrolled by Josiah Wedgwood, Beddoes founded the Pneumatic Institution for Inhalation Gas Therapy, which opened in Clifton,

The Millenium Clock in Shifnal.

near Bristol, in 1798, three years after Wedgwood's death. The institute applied the extension of the ideas of Joseph Priestley in the belief that disease could be medically treated by the therapeutic inhalation of different 'factious airs, gases, or vapours'. The apparatus for the treatment was designed and constructed in collaboration with James Watt. The institute advertised free treatment for those suffering from consumption, asthma, dropsy, obstinate venereal complaints, and scrofula.

Dr Beddoes employed the 20-year-old genius Humphry Davy as his first superintendent, who in 1799 discovered the properties of nitrous oxide (laughing gas). Davy left in 1801 to join the newly founded Royal Institute in London. The following year, 1802, Beddoes' Pneumatic Institution closed with a disillusioned Beddoes abandoning his original aims. Pneumatology was considered neither safe nor effective. The institute became a general hospital which Beddoes left in 1807, one year before his death in 1808, at the age of 48.

Thomas Beddoes was a radical well-intentioned philanthropist, a charismatic maverick doctor whose support for the French Revolution made him unpopular in many quarters. He was a member of the Lunar Society.

SHREWSBURY

~ Shropshire's Burning ~

Nestling within a great loop of the River Severn lies the county town of Shropshire – Shrewsbury, without doubt one of the most beautiful and historic towns in England.

On the walls of a number of the older buildings in Shrewsbury's town centre are various metal plaques, many of which date back to the eighteenth century. These are the emblems of insurance companies known as 'Fire Insurance Plaques', or 'Fire Marks'. The plaques are mostly made of lead or iron, but sometimes brass was used. They were fixed to the wall of a building so that the local fire company could identify which buildings were insured by a particular insurer.

In those days there was no municipal fire brigade; each insurance company maintained its own fire brigade, crews directly employed to attend fires at a building insured by their employer. The fire crew would, however, attempt to put out a fire at buildings that were insured by a different company, but only if the owner was able to agree a fee pretty sharpish with whichever fire crew turned up.

This practice was begun by the Sun Fire Office, established in 1710, and from there quickly spread around the country. The Salop Fire Office was established in 1780, enjoying a monopoly until 1837 when the Shropshire and North Wales Assurance Company was formed. The Salop Fire Office charged 8 shillings and 6 pence, unless transferring from another company in which case they were given a free policy. Their Fire Mark depicted the heads of three leopards – the arms of Shrewsbury. In 1890, this company united with the Alliance Assurance Company, and in 1906, the County Fire Office Limited was added to that company. The Alliance maintained the Salop Fire Brigade until 1918, when it was taken over by Shrewsbury Corporation, along with those at Bishop's Castle, Welshpool, and Bridgnorth Fire Brigades.

The fire engines were not the sleek red vehicles we see, and hear, today, but were horse-drawn engines which were unable to react as fast as might be desired; the horses had to be taken from their stalls and harnessed before they could set off. Shrewsbury's old fire station, No. 7, was located at Cross Hill Court, and the horses were kept at Franklin's Livery Stables at Cross Hill.

By around 1825, many fire companies had combined, making fire plaques unnecessary, and so they were seen more as advertisements rather than as identification marks. Many were left in place, as had some previously, even after an insurance policy had expired. In London the amalgamation and integration of many of these early fire brigades resulted in the entire city being served by one brigade, the London Fire Engine Establishment.

~ *The Lion Still Roars* ~

The Grade I listed sixteenth-century coaching inn, the Lion Hotel, on Shrewsbury's Wyle Cop, has seen much activity and has had many famous guests since it was first built in the 1770s. A former mayor and town clerk of Shrewsbury, John Ashby, had the hotel built, however, in 1779 he died, bankrupted by the cost of the project.

The famous Lion Hotel, Wyle Cop, Shrewsbury.

On Monday, 2 September 1831, 22-year-old Charles Darwin left the hotel for London, after learning that a second person had been offered the post of naturalist of the expedition on HMS *Beagle*, and feared he might miss the opportunity.

The great Italian composer and violin virtuoso Niccolo Paganini gave a concert in the Lion ballroom on 15 August 1833 – one of the great many celebrities that have been associated with the Lion Hotel.

Charles Dickens was a fairly frequent guest at the Lion, staying on 31 October 1838 with his then wife Catherine, to attend a performance of the play *A Roland for an Oliver* at the Shrewsbury Theatre. They left the following day to travel to Llangollen.

He also stayed at the Lion in May 1852. This time he was appearing in the comedy *Not So Bad as We Seem, Or, Many Sides to a Character: A Comedy in Five Acts*, by Sir Edward Bulwer-Lytton. The performance at the Shrewsbury Music Hall concluded with an original farce in one act titled 'Mr Nightingale's Diary', by the author himself in collaboration with Mark Lemon, the editor of the magazine *Punch*.

Newly separated from his wife, Dickens stayed again in August 1858 along with his friend, the great illustrator Hablot Knight Browne, better known as the cartoonist Phiz. Brown illustrated Dickens' *The Pickwick Papers*. The great author gave a reading at the Shrewsbury Music Hall of his novella *A Christmas Carol*.

Lodging in rooms that were then in an annexe, Dickens wrote of the hotel in a letter to one of his daughters:

> We have the strangest little rooms, the ceilings of which I can touch with my hand. The windows bulge out over the street as if they were the stern windows of a ship. And a door opens out of the sitting room on to a little gallery with plants in it where one leans over a queer old rail.

It has been said that whilst staying at the Lion, Dickens penned at least some of the *The Pickwick Papers*.

~ *Buried Alive* ~

In the 1780s, the graveyard of St Julian's church in Shrewsbury was the scene of a disturbing event, when a man, believed to be dead, was buried. The unfortunate victim was a cook staying at the Lion Hotel in Wyle Cop, by the name of Mr Taur, who one day fell down dead after a coughing fit. He was buried in the graveyard.

That night the sexton, along with nearby residents, heard cries coming from somewhere in the graveyard, but ignored them – initially putting the noises down to the sound of the wind, or the rustling of leaves. However, later on suspicions arose that something was amiss; so the newly buried coffin was dug up. When the cover was removed, to everyone's horror it was discovered the underside of the lid

St Julian's church, Fish Street, Shrewsbury, with St Alkmund's church in the background.

was scored with the marks of Mr Taur's scratches as he fought to claw himself free, and his fingers were worn down to the bone. It turned out that the cook had not died when he had collapsed, but had merely fallen into a coma. Mr Taur's spirit is said to haunt the Lion Hotel, along with a whole lot of other ghosts.

~ *The Ducking Pool* ~

Few people realise that in front of the Old Market Hall in Shrewsbury there was a marshy pool traditionally known as the Bishop's Pool, and it was here that the ducking or cucking stool, sometimes called the 'Stool of Repentance', was situated. The stool was used for ducking the perpetrators of minor offences against society, such as wives who nagged too much, or as punishment for dishonest traders, and was very much seen as public entertainment.

The ducking stool was also one of the instruments used to determine the guilt of any person accused of being a heretic or of being involved in witchcraft. The offender was brought to the Bishop's Pool and firmly strapped to a chair-like apparatus suspended on a sort of axle so that it always stayed upright; this in turn was attached to a long, sturdy wooden beam mounted on a seesaw type of arrangement. Sometimes two beams were fixed in parallel. Some ducking stools were mounted on wheels to enable them to be easily wheeled to the water's edge, others were hung from bridges.

The Old Market Hall, Shrewsbury.

The Saxons also used this method of punishment, when it was known as a 'scalding stole' (scalding stool). It is not certain when this kind of device was last used; some records suggest 1807 or 1808, but it appears that Shrewsbury Town Corporation purchased a new ducking stool in 1669.

~ *Selection? Naturally.* ~

The author of *The Origin of Species*, Shrewsbury's Charles Darwin, himself originated from good stock. His maternal grandfather was the famous potter and social reformer Josiah Wedgwood. His paternal grandfather was noted doctor and naturalist Erasmus Darwin, himself a larger-than-life character. Both men were instrumental in forming the famous Lunar Society, originally named the Lunar Circle, so-called because they would meet on the Monday night nearest the full moon, members gathering together for a lively dinner. A group of men with fertile minds that changed the world, the Lunarmen, as they were affectionately known

The statue of Charles Darwin, sitting proudly outside the entrance to Shrewsbury Library.

(incidentally, they called themselves 'Lunatics'), met in Birmingham at Soho House. This was the home of Matthew Boulton (1728–1809), the industrialist and flamboyant entrepreneur. Other members included the brilliant engineer, James Watt (1736–1819); radical polymath and discoverer of oxygen, Joseph Priestley (1733–1804); chemist, James Kerr (1735–1820) – who was the first man to make affordable soap; inventor and theorist, Richard Lovell Edgworth (1744–1817); the inventor of the gas light, William Murdock (1731–1802), who worked for Boulton and Watt; mathematician and philosopher, William Small (1734–1775), who was the mentor of Thomas Jefferson, third President of the United States. Small died aged 40, and was replaced by doctor and botanist William Withering (1741–1799), discoverer of digitalis (foxglove) as a treatment for heart disease.

The list of illustrious peripheral members reads like an eighteenth-century Who's Who of the brilliant and the famous, people such as Thomas Jefferson; Benjamin Franklin; Sir Richard Arkwright; Thomas Beddoes; Anna Seward; and John Smeaton.

~ *The Master of Mischief* ~

In Shrewsbury during medieval times, a gang of marauding Morris dancers often wandered the town, causing mayhem wherever they went. The leader of this mob was known by various names, ranging from the Master of Mischief; Lord of Misrule; the Abbot of Marham, or Mayroll, or Mardall, or Marall; and the Lord of Abbot Marram. Money towards the cost of costumes and minstrels was provided by Shrewsbury Corporation, and sometimes a bellman would be employed to go around the town to drum up interest.

~ *A Bridge Too Far* ~

On Christmas Day in 1752, those citizens of the town that resided on the Old Stone Bridge went off to church not knowing of the catastrophe that was to befall their humble homes, for when they returned they found that their homes had disappeared, having fallen into the River Severn when part of the bridge collapsed. The seventeen-arch Stone Bridge was an ancient structure with thirty-three houses and shops on the parapet, and at one end was guarded by a strong tower. Apparently a couple of beams collapsed, spilling the houses into the river. The sad event became known as the 'Christmas Mishap'.

The name Stone Bridge derives from medieval times, when this Norman bridge incorporated fortifications and a drawbridge. It collapsed in 1546, and was rebuilt. The 1774 version opened but was found to be too narrow for modern traffic; it was also steep, with a hump in the centre of the span to allow masted boats to pass underneath. The bridge was completely rebuilt in 1927, reusing the old stonework.

~ *Shrewsbury's Ship Money* ~

The medieval tax known as Ship Money was reinstated in 1634, without the approval of Parliament, when King Charles I's attorney, searching for some means of wiping out the royal debt of £1,200,000, discovered among the records in the Tower of London papers from the time of the Plantagenet kings. The documents gave details of a former decree that in times of war the cost of provisioning ships and their equipment could be levied on seaboard towns and maritime counties; this tax was known as Ship Money. How much this astute discovery meant to King Charles I may have to be judged from the financial results. By way of establishing some scale to this, in the year 1635, the ordinary revenue of the Crown amounted to £600,000, but Ship Money alone brought in £104,000, and by extending the writs demanding Ship Money to inland towns in 1635, the receipts were doubled. This unwelcome tax flew in the face of several statutes, confirming the conditions set out in Magna Carta, that made it illegal for the levying of any taxes without the consent of Parliament. It was one more grievance against the growing mood in the country of dissatisfaction with the king. Remember Charles had dismissed Parliament in 1629, beginning eleven years of personal rule.

At first the writs were issued only to seaboard towns, although the wording of these documents was carefully drawn up to avoid any statement that might provide inland towns with a claim to immunity. The first writ issued says, significantly:

> ... enough and although that charge of defence which concerned all men ought to be supported by all as by the laws and customs of the kingdom of England have been accustomed to be done. Not commonly withstanding we considering that you constituted in the sea coasts are chiefly bound to set your helping hand.

In August 1635, Shrewsbury was called upon to contribute £456 10*s*, a large sum when compared with the amounts levied upon several other towns. For example, Wenlock was asked to pay £302, Coventry £266, Bridgnorth £61 10*s*, Winchester £119, Stafford a mere £30, Canterbury £300, and Hereford £220. Only one community was asked to contribute more than Shrewsbury, and that was Gloucester, who were asked to pay £500 – it should be remembered that in those days Gloucester was a vast port city with many great churches and a great minster. The total demanded from the county of Shropshire was £4,500, compared with Staffordshire £2,000, Warwickshire £4,000, Lancashire £3,500, Northamptonshire £6,000, and Somersetshire £8,000.

Before the end of the year the bailiffs of Shrewsbury were protesting against their assessment on the grounds that, firstly, it should be in accordance with the customary proportion of the town's contribution to public charges on the whole country, secondly, that the ravages of the plague had impoverished the town, and thirdly that the sheriff's methods of assessment were unfair. The town's usual share of county charges claimed the bailiff's part was one-fifteenth-and-a-half, and therefore the correct sum for them to pay should be £292 10*s*. Moreover, even this would be difficult to collect as the ravages of the plague had severely depleted the finances of the borough. This was no mere appeal to sentiment; the law demanded that poor sufferers should be relieved by rates. There was plague in Shrewsbury in 1631, and in that outbreak the town suffered severely, particularly in the parishes of St John's and St Chad's, so much so that the corporation of Bishop's Castle had instigated a voluntary collection for the relief of Shrewsbury sufferers, raising £16.

The Ship Money Act was declared legal by twelve judges in 1637; it was urgent that naval defence should be provided against the Turks and all other pirates in those troublesome times. In 1639, it was fast becoming apparent that the organisation for the collection of Ship Money was breaking down. Towns everywhere were in arrears with payments, and the threats made by the Court of the Star Chamber were either ignored or met with half-hearted excuses as to why the arrears were not forthcoming; less than 20 per cent of the money demanded was paid. Shrewsbury was definitely in arrears and no effective measures were being taken to wipe them off, although the mayor of the town was personally threatened in a letter that he received from London. The Ship Money tax was declared illegal by the Long Parliament in 1641.

~ *Shrews and Witches* ~

In earlier times the Catholic Church placed the practice of witchcraft on the same level as heresy, citing that in effect it was the same as worshipping the devil or false gods. As a result, anyone accused of being a witch could look forward to being subjected to all manner of painful degradation. The rise of Calvinism resulted in an increase in the number of accusations of witchcraft. Puritans appeared to revel in the spectacle of witch trials and of the resultant treatment metered out on the unfortunate victims of the pointed finger.

The sixteenth and seventeenth centuries saw no respite for poor old women who lived alone and owned a black cat; two notoriously accurate signs of being a witch. But of course the accusers didn't just pick on old women for their persecution, in fact anyone, male or female, was considered to be fair game by these God-fearing accusers, as long as their victims met the desired criteria. It was not just the common people who held these beliefs: King James I, himself a Calvinist, firmly believed in the existence of witchcraft, and in 1604 an Act of Parliament was passed which made the practice of witchcraft an offence. A group of Charlatans developed, known as Witchmongers, who professed an ability to identify witches. The Act was repealed in 1752, following the drowning of a woman in Tring, Hertfordshire.

~ A Big Curious White Elephant ~

This is a curious tale of a bad investment, in fact, two – both very much seen as white elephants. The first was the Armoury, a lovely building which today stands at Victoria Quay near the Welsh Bridge. It is currently a busy restaurant enjoyed by diners, few who realise the curious history of the building.

The Armoury was built in 1806, at the instigation of a controversial younger son of the Earl of Tankerville, Henry Grey Bennet, MP for Shrewsbury, at a cost of around £10,000. Designed by James Wyatt to store up to 25,000 pieces of ordnance, such as muskets of the various local militias of Shropshire and the surrounding counties, the site also housed two gunpowder stores, plus a few outbuildings. Local military men poured scorn on the project, citing that it was too far from military barracks to be defended, and as most of the local militia units were away at the Napoleonic Wars there was no need for such a store. Very few weapons were ever stored at the Armoury, and later the Shropshire Militia stored their weapons in Shrewsbury's Market Hall at a cost of £45 per year. Incidentally, the Tankervilles sold the land on which the Armoury was built to the Crown for £400.

In 1827, the building was purchased by William Hazledine for £2,700, who rented out the other buildings for housing, the Armoury remaining empty. Hazledine sold it in 1835, for £3,292, to Lord Berwick, whose grand plan was to convert the building into luxury accommodation for customers paying to take the waters at his nearby Sutton Spa. Sadly the flow of the salty, iron-flavoured water was never fast enough to make the spa a going concern, and so despite heavy investments on baths and walls, the project never really got off the ground.

The Armoury, Victoria Quay, Shrewsbury.

The Armoury remained empty and unused until it was sold to the Shropshire Assizes for £5,000, ironically for the use of the Shropshire Militia, who stayed until 1880, when they moved to new barracks at Copthorn. The next thirty years saw the building used for musical entertainments. In 1914, the building was used to house Belgian refugees of the First World War. Following the end of the war, when there was a shortage of building materials, Morris' Bakery purchased the building, moving it lock, stock and barrel from its site between London Road and Wenlock Road to its current home at Victoria Quay. In 1995, it was converted into a restaurant.

SHROPSHIRE

The county of Shropshire has many weird customs. Here are just a couple.

~ Riding the Stang ~

This rather curious old custom concerns the local community taking matters of social conscience into its own hands, a tradition that was still to be found in Shropshire at the turn of the twentieth century.

If a local couple caused scandal by their infidelity or by their constant quarrelling, the community might show its disapproval by the rowdy demonstration known as 'Riding the Stang.'

Effigies, called 'Mawkins', of the offending couple were made, usually from sacking stuffed with straw, much like Guys on Bonfire Night. These would be lashed to long poles called 'Stangs', which would be paraded around the village or town, in and out of streets, swelling the numbers of the crowd of vigilantes whistling, banging pots and pans, and yelling doggerel verses about the offending couple. Eventually the mob would arrive in front of the home of the culprits where they would flourish the effigies in the air, repeating the shouting and the general commotion from the parade. The demonstration would end with the 'Mawkins' being burnt on a hastily constructed bonfire in front of the culprits' house, or as near as was safe. The couple would be left in no doubt of the local community's disapproval of their behaviour.

~ Selling the Wife ~

This custom was not restricted to Shropshire: the practice of wife selling was rife all over the country, and Thomas Hardy included it in his *The Mayor of Casterbridge.*

In older times when there was not much money around, it was not unusual to find a man who wanted to sell his wife, for although legal divorce has been widely available in this country for many centuries, the fees for legal services were often prohibitive, particularly to those in the lower classes of society. The alternative to an expensive divorce was to sell your wife, which was widely believed to be acceptable and perfectly legal – because in those days it was the custom for a wife to be thought of as the property of her husband. Any such sale, however, must be seen to be done in both a public and formal manner. The husband of the wife to be sold must lead her to the market place by a halter which was fastened about her neck. On occasion it was the done thing to hire the services of the Town Crier to call out notice of the sale in advance, thus making sure that there was a sufficiently large crowd of witnesses to the correctness of the proceedings. In many cases a legal contract was drawn up, the wording of which would go something like, 'We the undersigned agree to part wholly and solely for life, and not to trouble one another for life'. Sometimes additional conditions were included, depending on the situation and circumstances of the husband and wife. To be sold so publicly must have been a most humiliating experience for even the most hard-hearted woman.

It was recorded that in Shropshire, on her way to the market place, the wife to be sold had to first pass through the gate of a turnpike. The price to purchase her was set at 5 shillings plus a quart of ale. The price in other such sales have been reported as being as low as 1 shilling, and others at £1 4*s* plus a bowl of punch.

STANTON LACY

~ The Disgraced Vicar ~

This is the tale of a disgraced clergyman named Robert Foulkes. He was born on 19 February 1633/34, in Mallwyd in Wales, and was baptised on 19 March 1633/34, later attending the Royal Free Grammar School at Shrewsbury. In 1651, Foulkes became a servitor of Christ Church in Oxford, continuing there for four years, subsequently becoming a preacher.

A note of clarification is needed here regarding the above dates. Before the adoption of the Gregorian calendar in 1752, the civil and legal start of the new year was on Lady Day, 25 March. The last day of the old year was therefore 24 March. So, what these days would be called 31 January 1679, was regarded as still being 1678. To avoid confusion, it was often referred to, and written down, as 31 January 1678/79.

Back to our story. On 7 September 1657, Foulkes married Isabella Colbatch at Ludlow parish church. Isabella's deceased father was a former rector of Stanton Lacy church, near Ludlow. Three years after their marriage, on 12 September 1660, Foulkes was himself appointed vicar at Stanton Lacy. Their union was blessed with four children, all born between 1665 and 1673.

Following the death of her father in 1637, Isabella had been raised in the household of Thomas Atkinson, who had succeeded her father as rector, and who on 8 April 1657 had died – the year she married Robert Foulkes.

The Revd Atkinson had a daughter, Ann Atkinson, born around 1650. She was a girl of considerable fortune, who was still an infant when her father died, and had been committed to the care of Robert Foulkes, who was then seen as a man of high moral principle by the executors of her father's will.

However, instead of providing the girl with good Christian instruction and guidance, as she grew older Foulkes introduced her to the licentious pleasures of the flesh. She was apparently more than willing to accept his sexual advances, and all too easily agreed to gratify his lust.

Gossipmongers in the village had it that Foulkes was messing around with this girl. Unfortunately there is no information about when their affair began, only that it was certainly going on in 1669, when he was reported as having been seen publically misbehaving with the young lady, kissing, fondling and embracing; it was around this time that Foulkes became a frequenter of local inns and was known as a heavy drinker.

Rumours of infidelity were rife when in 1674, Ann, now a 23-year-old woman, was sent away to West Felton, near Oswestry, to the home of Edward Walker, who had been a neighbour of her elder brother, Francis Atkinson, in Stanton Lacy. It was there on 6 May that she gave birth to a baby girl, also named Ann. The baby was rumoured to have been fostered to a couple living in Llansanffraid, Monmouthshire, and raised as Mary Morris. It was never conclusively proved that Foulkes was the father of the child, despite a series of allegations to the contrary.

St Peter's church, Stanton Lacy.

After the birth, Ann Atkinson returned briefly to Stanton Lacy, and a short time later she was packed off to her uncle's house in Claverley, near Bridgnorth, then finally to London where she resided with a kinsman of her family.

Some time later Ann returned to Stanton Lacy, and in the summer of 1676, following a new series of complaints about Foulkes' continuing relationship with her, coupled with other misbehaviours, he was brought before a Diocean Consistory Court in Ludlow on 1 August 1676. This resulted in Foulkes receiving a severe admonishment from Herbert Croft, the Bishop of Hereford. Consistory Courts heard cases of moral misdemeanours such as fornication before marriage, adultery, incest, blasphemy, and bad behaviour in church. These courts were abolished by Oliver Cromwell's Commonwealth, but restored in 1661.

It was also revealed that when Foulkes was drunk he became extremely aggressive. One day he assaulted his wife, beating her so savagely that Joan Wood, a maid servant who witnessed the violent attack, ran to get help, fetching the Constable's deputy and Richard Cherme, a yeoman farmer and churchwarden, who tried to stop the vicar. Foulkes attacked the churchwarden, knocking him downstairs and hitting him on the elbow and shoulder with a pair of tongs.

Foulkes' affair with Ann Atkinson continued under the nose of his wife until the young lady became pregnant again. Knowing that his reputation would not survive a second series of allegations, and all other options exhausted, Foulkes took rooms in York Buildings in London's Strand, and moved the girl in. He refused to allow anyone to help, and delivered the child himself. Unfortunately for the vicar, local women heard Ann's cries of pain and suspected that something was amiss. The babe was born on 16 January 1678, and Foulkes returned to Shropshire the next day.

The shocking fact that the child had been murdered came to light soon after; its body had been cruelly disposed of. Foulkes' villainous actions proved to have been a botched job, for the body was found and foul play suspected. When Foulkes was interviewed by the authorities he made a full confession, as did Ann.

The case was tried at the Old Bailey in London on 16 January 1678/79, and Robert Foulkes was found guilty of murder; Ann was acquitted. There were other allegations that Foulkes had cut the baby's throat with a knife, others that he had strangled the newborn. Some believed that Foulkes had paid to have the evil deed done rather than by his own hand.

In prison the condemned man displayed great penitence and regret, finding the time to write a bestselling pamphlet while waiting for his execution, titled 'An Alarme For Sinners'. Foulkes also received visits from a number of high-ranking ecclesiastics.

Robert Foulkes was executed at Tyburn on the morning of 31 January 1679, and, having danced the 'Tyburn jg', was buried at St Giles-in-the-Fields.

STOKE ST MILBOROUGH

~ *Well Well* ~

Earlier, we heard the legendary story of St Milburga's Well. Milburga was the eldest daughter of King Merewald of Magonsaete and his wife Queen Ermenburga, herself a saint. Milburga was reputedly beautiful and pious, and as we know founded a monastery for religious virgins at Wenlock where she was abbess. This is the legend of how her holy well at Stoke St Milborough got its name.

Abbess Milburga was not the kind of person to sit around praying all day, but preferred to travel around the countryside doing good works. Noted for her humility, she was endowed with the gift of healing, even restoring sight to the blind. Legend has it that the beautiful Milburga had many enemies, probably those who still followed the pagan religion.

One day, word came that her enemies were on their way to get her. Milburga escaped capture by taking flight on a white horse (some say it was an ass) and she spurred away to get a head start. Her pursuing foes had with them a pack of howling bloodhounds, plus a gang of ruffians.

After two days and nights of hard riding, Milburga reached the spot where the well named after her now is, and fell, exhausted, from her horse, striking her head on a stone. Blood flowed freely from the wound and the bloodstain it left upon the stone remained there plainly visible.

In a field opposite, known locally as Plock's Field, some men sowing barley saw her fall and ran to help. They needed water to bathe her wound but none was at hand or nearby. While the men were trying to decide what to do, Milburga recovered consciousness and without delay bade her horse strike the stone with its hoof, which the horse did, and immediately a spring of water gushed out of the rock. 'Holy water, henceforth, and forever flow freely,' said Milburga. She then stretched out her hands towards the field from whence the sowers had come, and commanded the barley the men had just sown to spring up; instantly green shoots appeared from the soil. Turning to the men, she told them that her pursuers were close at hand, and would presently ask them, 'When did the lady on the white horse pass this way?' They were to answer, 'When we were sowing the barley.'

Milburga then remounted her horse, thanked the men for their help, and bid them to prepare their sickles, for in the evening of that very day they should cut the barley. She went on her way, leaving the men perplexed and amazed at the miracle they had witnessed.

Later that evening, exactly as Milburga had predicted, the barley had grown and was ready for cutting. The men gathered up their sickles and scythes and set about their work. While they were busy reaping, Milburga's enemies rode up and asked for news of her. The men replied as she had asked them to, saying they had seen her when they were sowing the barley. The pursuers looked at the field and saw only a mass of tall barley. Baffled, Milburga's enemies rode back from where they came.

Another story tells that while Milburga was out doing good work, she was spied by a neighbouring prince, who, taken by her beauty, determined to make her his bride. Again she rode away to escape the prince's clutches, fording the River Corve. As soon as Milburga had reached the opposite bank, the river swelled to an impassable raging torrent, forcing the prince to give up the chase. In another tale, Milburga raised a child from the dead, although there are scant details of this tale.

T

TONG

~ Murder Most Horrid ~

Tong is a lovely little hamlet situated just off the A41. Anyone travelling in a northerly direction from junction 3 of the M54 must marvel at the beauty of its magnificent fifteenth-century church. Dedicated to St Bartholomew, it is a fine example of a battlemented church with its landmark octagonal tower and spire, which houses the largest bell in Shropshire, the Great Bell of Tong. At night the church is illuminated, and is a magical sight to behold.

Not far from the church once stood Tong Castle, which was demolished in the 1950s to make way for the construction of the M54 motorway, however, curious stories still abound.

One such story concerns the death of a maid who worked at the castle in the 1800s, and whose lifeless body was discovered in the ornamental water feature in the castle grounds, with blood oozing from her nostrils. The manner of her

The church of St Bartholomew at Tong.

death was the cause of much suspicion, and foul play was suspected. In those days the squire of the castle was known as a bit of an eccentric fellow, as anyone who has seen pictures of the peculiar design of the buildings would surely testify. He decided to invoke an age-old custom to determine the identity of the culprit, and so had all the people of the house – his family, servants and retainers – line up, and one by one walk to the corpse and touch it, in order that he might observe their reaction. The belief in Shropshire was that any person who laid hands on the corpse of a murdered person and shrank away would have violent nightmares featuring the dead person, so vivid that they would expose themselves as the murderer, whether the evil deed had been committed using violence or if spells had been used.

In the case at Tong Castle, the squire believed the sight of the bloody nose of the victim might shock the murderer into revealing themselves. Unfortunately in this case, the old ways did not work.

~ Little Nell ~

The graveyard at St Bartholomew's church at Tong is the site of 'Little Nell's' grave. This curious tomb came about because of one of Charles Dickens' many connections to Shropshire. He reputedly set the closing chapters of *The Old Curiosity Shop* in the graveyard of Tong church, where lies the grave of 'Little Nell' – and lo and behold such a grave appeared, but why would a fictitious character have an actual grave? Following the serialisation of the story in England, the story was then successfully published in the USA, its popularity so enormous

The grave of Little Nell, Tong.

that American visitors to Shropshire wanted to see the grave for themselves. Not wanting to miss out on the profits of tourism, the residents of Tong contributed to a fund to pay for a headstone – and thus everyone was happy. It is suggested that Dickens visited Tong when his grandmother worked at Tong Castle.

There is another faux Dickens grave in Shropshire. This one is in the graveyard of St Chad's church in Shrewsbury. The grave of Ebenezer Scrooge, a prop in the 1984 film version of the classic *A Christmas Carol*, starring George C. Scott, was left behind when the film crew departed.

U

UPTON MAGNA

~ How TT Kept Us in Suspension ~

Upton Forge and the Forge Farmhouse lie a short distance from the quiet and peaceful village of Upton Magna, a few miles east of Shrewsbury. Today the farmhouse is an unassuming Grade II listed building, however, in the late eighteenth and early nineteenth centuries this site was a hive of industrial activity. It was here in 1821 that the owner of Upton Forge, the great Shropshire industrialist William Hazledine, was contracted to manufacture high-quality, wrought-iron chain bars for Thomas Telford's marvellous suspension bridge over the Menai Straits, from the Bangor in North Wales to Porthaethwy on the island of Anglesey.

The wrought-iron chain bars were forged at Upon Forge and then taken, together with connecting plates, to Hazledine's Coleham foundry and engineering works in Shrewsbury for finishing. They were transported along the now disused Shrewsbury Canal, which the forge stood alongside. Two bad winters, in 1822/23 and 1823/24, produced floods at the forge which severely hampered the project, however in the end the order was fulfilled, the wrought iron being subjected to rigorous testing before passed for use.

The Menai Suspension Bridge (*Pont y Borth* in Welsh) has sixteen massive chains to support the structure, each 1,714ft long and weighing 121 tons, each made up of 935 wrought-iron bars. This monumental feat of engineering opened on 30 January 1826, construction having begun in 1819. To avoid rusting, the iron was soaked in linseed oil and later painted. In 1938, the original iron chains were replaced with steel chains.

Upton Forge was still producing in 1831; that's when it appears to have been last mentioned in any written work However, William Hazledine's foundry in Shrewsbury continued to operate after its owner's death in 1840. Upton Forge was one of the last rural forges to close. Its isolated location and the smallness of its operation, together with investment in new production techniques, made it eventually unsustainable.

Quaint Cruck Cottage, Upton Magna.

~ It's Cruck, Mate ~

Upton Magna village also lays claim to the oldest cottage in Europe still standing, well part of it anyway. Cruck Cottage is a picturesque, chocolate-box vision of quaintness, with its attractive thatched roof and timber-framed construction. Tests on the timber structure indicate a date of 1269.

V

VIROCONIUM

~ What the Romans Did For Us ~

The Roman city of Viroconium Cornoviorum, also known as *Uriconium*, began life as a small auxiliary legionary fort. Dated to the Julio–Claudian period around AD 47, the fort was probably built by the First Cohort of Thracians to protect the ford across the River Severn, close to the present-day village of Wroxeter. The site lies about 5 miles east-south-east of Shrewsbury, built on land belonging to the ancient Briton tribe, the Cornovii. Over time the site was developed into the fourth largest civilian settlement in Roman Britain, reputedly larger than Roman London, covering an area of 200 acres, with a population of around 6,000 at its peak (some put this figure at nearly 15,000), including many retired legionnaires and traders.

Although nowhere near fully excavated, Viroconium has been described as one of the best examples of second-century town planning. The Latin name *Uriconium* translates from a form of the Celtic word *Uiroconion*, meaning 'place of the man-wolf'.

The Old Work, Viroconium, at Wroxeter.

The village of Wroxeter occupies a corner of part of the southern end of the settlement. It was partly built by the Saxons using stone taken from the old Roman town, evidence of which can be seen at many places around the village. The entrance to the church is flanked by two Roman pillars, and inside the church the great font has been fashioned from the base of a Roman pillar turned upside down.

The Romans invaded Britain in earnest in AD 43, when the Emperor Claudius sent Aulus Plautius, first Governor of Britannia, with four legions comprising around 40,000 men (20,000 legionaires plus auxilliaries) from Gaul, following an appeal for help from an ousted tribal ally. The Romans were undoubtedly attracted by the material wealth of Britannia. After the initial successful invasion, Emperor Claudius travelled across the Channel to accept the surrender of the defeated chieftains. He stayed for sixteen days before returning to Gaul. The offensive, which began in the south, gradually spread northwards, and soon reached the West Midlands. Late in AD 47, the new governor, Publius Ostorius Scapula, commenced a campaign against the tribes of Wales and what is now Cheshire. Ostorius died in AD 52, and was succeeded by Aulus Didius Gallus.

At Viroconium, the Thracians were relieved by the XIV Germina legion, and by about AD 57 the first major components of the settlement were established. In AD 58, Emperor Nero decreed that the imperial boundaries of his empire needed to be secured, and a larger legionary fortress was constructed. Nero wanted the tribes of mid-Wales and North Wales to be subjugated, and over the next twenty years Viroconium became very much a military base. The XIV were replaced, in AD 69, by the XX Valeria Victrix legion. By AD 88, the military base had become more of a supply depot, and by AD 90 had been abandoned by the fighting legions following the establishment of a new legionary fortress in Deva (Chester).

Reconstruction of a Roman Villa at Viroconium, Wroxeter.

Over time, Viroconium became the hub of the Cornovian territory, a *civitas*, known now as Viroconium Cornoviorum. However, following the withdrawal from Britain of the last of the Roman legions in AD 408, Britain's tribes, now at the mercy of invaders from Saxony, were left to their own devices.

The next couple of centuries saw the city gradually run down, and apart from the village of Wroxeter, it was finally abandoned in the seventh and eighth centuries.

Centuries of farming and stone-robbing has decimated much of the site, part of which has undergone a series of archaeological investigations to expose a good portion of what was once the centre of the city. One piece of masonry, known as the Old Work, survived above ground level. It is the best preserved section of the *insula* (town baths), and the tallest free-standing Roman structure in Britain; it was originally planned as the Flavian *forum basilica*, but was incorporated into the Hadrianic bath-suite. The site is owned and run by English Heritage and is well worth a visit.

W

WELLINGTON

~ Digitalis ~

The year 1741 saw the birth of a man who was instrumental in the discovery of digitalis as an aid in the treatment of heart disease. William Withering (17 March 1741–6 October 1799) was born in Wellington, Shropshire, the only son of surgeon Edmund Withering. Young William was apprenticed to his father in 1758, before attending Edinburgh University in 1762, where he studied medicine, qualifying as a doctor three years later. His first appointment was in 1766 in Stafford, as one of the first doctors at the newly founded infirmary. He married Helena Cooke in 1772, the union being blessed with a son and a daughter.

Withering's interest in botany drew him to investigate heart disease. A chance meeting with a woman selling homemade cures prompted him to investigate the properties and uses of foxglove (*digitalis purpurea*). He systematically experimented, and finally published in 1785 'An Account of the Foxglove and some of its Medical Uses; with practical remarks on the dropsy, and some other diseases', which introduced digitalis as a drug for cardiac disease.

He remained in Stafford until 1775, when he took over the Birmingham medical practice of Dr William Small, who had been physician to the illustrious industrialist Matthew Boulton, with whom he became friends, joining the famous Lunar Society.

Withering was subsequently appointed Chief Physician at the newly established Birmingham General Hospital, and held that position for thirteen years.

In 1784, Withering was elected a Fellow of the Royal Society for his work in mineralogy. He wrote numerous books and papers on the subjects of medicine, mineralogy and botany. A painstaking experimenter, specifically on the subject of heart disease, he is up there with the important pioneers of medicine. He was also a translator of many foreign works, and in 1792 discovered that 'fairy rings' were caused by the roots of mushrooms.

William Withering FRS died in 1799. He was buried at Edgbaston Old Church, where there is a lasting memorial to his memory, which includes an engraving of a foxglove.

~ A Quick Dip ~

Until the 1940s, it was the custom in Wellington on Good Friday to douke or dip one's head in the stone cistern containing clear spring water from St Margaret's well. The well is situated in a field still known as Margaret's Well Field. The water is chalybeate water, strongly impregnated with sulphate of iron, and popularly believed to be a good treatment for the improvement of weak eyesight.

WELSHAMPTON

~ The African Prince ~

In the graveyard of St Michael and All Angels' church in Welshampton an African prince is interred. Prince Jeremiah Libopua Moshueshue (1839–63) was the son of King Moshueshu I of Lesotho, a southern African country formerly known as Basutuland. The young prince had been sent to England to train as a missionary at Canterbury.

Welshampton's connection with Lesotho came about when the vicar of the church, the Revd Thomas Buckley-Owen, was offered a post in Lesotho by the bishop of Orange River. It was a position he refused because he wanted to remain in Welshampton until the work on the building of his church has been completed. However, he did maintain contact with the bishop.

St Michael and All Angels' church, Welshampton.

When the church was complete, the prince accepted an invitation to attend the consecration ceremony of the church in 1863, but sadly whilst in Shropshire he caught a fever and died.

In 2010, Her Majesty Queen Masenate Mohato Seesio of Lesotho came to Welshampton to visit her ancestor's grave, accompanied by the High Commissioner Prince Seesio and Princess Mabereng Seesio.

~ Disaster on the Rails ~

One of the worst railway disasters in Shropshire happened near Welshampton Station at around 10.20 p.m. on 11 June 1897; it became known as the Welshampton train disaster. The train, a fifteen-carriage, two-locomotive excursion, was travelling from Barmouth on the Welsh coast. Departing at 6 p.m., the train carried 320 passengers from the resort to their home in Royton, near Oldham in Lancashire. The trip was the annual wakes excursion for seven Royton Sunday schools, who had began their journey at 2 a.m. that fateful morning, all excited at the prospect of a day out at the seaside.

All was fine until the train passed through Welshampton Station, when suddenly and without warning thirteen carriages left the track, tearing up around 300 yards of rails and sleepers.

Nine passengers were killed in the disaster, eight of them aged between 17 and 20 years. Two others and one railway employee died subsequently from their injuries. Survivors described how the train had been smashed to smithereens, with parts of carriages thrown over nearby hedgerows to litter the adjacent field.

The Old Station House plaque, Welshampton.

The majority of those unhurt in the accident travelled home the following day, leaving behind fifty of the injured in hospitals in Oswestry and Whitchurch.

The Board of Trade inquiry placed most of the blame on the condition of the small forty-year-old, four-wheeled brake van, which on the return journey was at the front of the train; the speed of the train may also have been too excessive for the state of the track, which had some sleepers that were in need of replacement. This resulted in compensation payments exceeding £8,000, paid by the Cambrian Rail Company.

Two memorials to the dead were placed near the scene of the accident: one, by local residents, at the side of the Ellesmere to Whitchurch road, the A495; the other, made of black granite with the names of the victims inscribed on it, outside Royton Town Hall.

The rail line was closed years later and Welshampton Station no longer sees trains whizzing past, for it is now a house.

WENLOCK EDGE

~ The Clattering Glat ~

The curiously named glat in question was a gap, or space, in the hedge or fence bounding a coppice on the road that runs along the Wenlock Edge, from Much Wenlock to Church Stretton, near to the local landmark known as Ippikin's Rock. This is the spot where an ancient pathway passes over the steep face of the cliff leading into Apedale. Sadly, history does not record the origin of why the gap was given the name Clattering.

The spot is where a great many years ago a foul murder took place. A son killed his father on the adjacent road, then in an attempt to conceal the crime dragged the body through the glat and into the coppice, covering the glat with thorn branches. The next day the blockage in the glat was discovered and removed, exposing the dead body. From that day forward, legend has it that whenever the glat is covered, it would be reopened the following night by fairies.

WESTON RHYN

~ A Most Barbaric War Crime ~

On the western fringes of Weston Rhyn there is a pretty narrow lane, flanked on one side by a stone-built wall, and on the other by a hedgerow – all very attractive. However, there are times when this lane and others nearby are not so nice, for then they are the scene of a scary haunting, the result of a barbaric war crime. A lady dressed in white is seen walking alone or sometimes riding in a phantom coach drawn by four grey/white horses.

The barbaric war crime in question took place towards the end of the First English Civil War, when the good citizens of Weston Rhyn, supporters of the Royalist cause, steadfastly refused to pay the taxes imposed upon them by Parliament. The puritan authorities in Shrewsbury reacted to this act of defiance by dispatching a troop of Roundhead soldiers to the village to collect the taxes due.

Upon their arrival, they wasted no time in rounding up the villagers and herding them to one central point. Faced with a troop of well-drilled and well-armed soldiers, the villages still refused to pay. The ruthless officer in command gave the order to his troopers to build a huge bonfire, which they did, and after this was done a large cauldron of water was placed on top, and the fire lit.

The water soon bubbled and boiled, and when it was scalding hot, a startled Miss Phillips, the owner of Tyn-y-Rhos Hall, was grabbed and lifted by the troopers, then unceremoniously lowered into the boiling water. Imagine her screams as she was boiled alive. However, after only a short time, still alive but in great pain, she was hauled out of the cauldron and thrown into the cold water of a nearby stream.

The villagers had seen enough: the Roundhead's savage act of inhumane cruelty broke their resistance. They handed over the taxes as prescribed. Not only that, but they surrendered a Catholic priest who had taken refuge nearby. Miss Phillips and the priest were then bound with ropes and marched away to Chirk Castle, where both prisoners were summarily executed.

Soon after this brutal event, the ghost of Miss Phillips began haunting the lanes near her home.

WHITCHURCH

~ The Black Death ~

On 20 August 1349, John Le Strange of Whitchurch died of the Black Death. Eight days later John's eldest son, Fulk Le Strange, and his brother, Humphrey Le Strange, both fell victim to the disease. The Black Death arrived in Shropshire around the spring of 1349, having arrived in the south of England in the summer of 1348. By September of that year it had spread to London, and thence to a large part of the country by the new year.

The disease had three basic strains: Bubonic plague; Pneumonic plague; and Septicaemic plague. The body of a victim would be covered in red spots, which would eventually cover the entire body; over time the spots turned black in colour, followed by death soon after, giving rise to the name 'Black Death'.

In Shropshire there are a host of medieval villages that were abandoned for one reason or another. Many give the reason as being the arrival of the Black Death, but of course this was not the only reason. During the fourteenth century the population was devastated by a series of failed harvests, resulting in villages being abandoned for economic reasons.

The name 'Black Death' struck fear and dread into the hearts of the people, rich and poor alike, because the disease was no respecter of wealth or position, and it took a vicious toll on the population. The belief is that the disease was spread by fleas carried on rats.

WHITTINGTON

~ Fulk Fitz Warine ~

The wonderfully atmospheric Whittington Castle, in Whittington, near Oswestry, is surrounded in legend, and is the catalyst for three romantic stories involving larger-than-life characters from one Norman family: the Fitz Warines. Sadly, historians have left us with many anomolies, frequently mixing up names and dates regarding the stories about the various Fulk Fitz Warines. Despite this, the stories are still worth including.

Following his success at the Battle of Hastings, William the Conqueror pressed on decisively with his subjugation of the Saxon population by awarding land and estates to his loyal vassals, such as Roger de Montgomery, first Earl of Shrewsbury, who built the castle at Whittington in the eleventh century, originally as a motte and bailey castle. Another of the Conqueror's faithful knights was Payn (Pagan)

The gatehouse of Whittington Castle.

Peverel, one time standard bearer for the Conqueror's eldest son, Robert Curthose, during the crusade of 1096–1100. Peverel was rewarded with lands across the Midlands and in Nottinghamshire. Payn Peverel was described as being one of the noblest sons of chivalry.

The area near Oswestry, which we know today as Whittington, passed into the Peverel family during the reign of King Henry I. The name derives from White Plain and from the construction of a White Tower, by William Peverel, which over time morphed into Whittington.

One of the castles the Peverels built was near a spot now known as Castleton in the Peak District, the castle being known as Peveril Castle of the Peaks. On Payn's death his estates passed to his nephew, William Peverel, who himself had no male issue. However, he had two nieces, Eleyne and Melette. William decided to provide dowries, and Melette's was to be Whittington.

Legend has it that Melette was a very beautiful but wilful young lady who constantly refused the advances of the many suitors her uncle recommended. Finally, at his wit's end, William determined that he would see her settled in marriage, and so organised a grand two-day tournament to be held in the meadows below Peveril Castle, to which the most eligible bachelor knights were invited. The victor's prize was to be the hand of the lovely Melette, plus the estates of Whittington and its castle. The great and good accepted the challenge, including at least three princes who rode in with a host of accompanying knights as part of their entourage.

The first day was reputed to be chaotic as the competitors proceeded to knock seven bells out of each other, however, this had the effect of sorting the men from the boys, with those left standing qualifying for day two. Melette had spotted her favourite, a knight by the name of Guarin de Metz (Warine), a cousin to the Duke of Brittany, who had arrived with ten of the duke's sons. She sent him her favour in the form of a glove with a message to defend her honour.

When the blood and gore had been cleared away, Guarin de Metz was declared the winner. He and Melette were married, and moved into the White Tower.

There is much speculation about the parentage of William Peverel, which adds an intriguing dynamic to the story. Some say that he was the illegitimate son of the Conqueror, whom Payn Peverel raised as his own, and that the title 'Defender of the Holy Grail' passed from the Conqueror to William. Somehow this title then passed to Melette, and thence to her husband, adding to the legend that the resting place of the Holy Grail is in a secret box somewhere in Whittington Castle. Guarin and Melette had a son whom they named Fulk. Fulk I Fitz Warine in turn had a son who he named Fulk II Fitz Warine.

~ Fulk Saves the Day ~

This second romantic tale includes an act of daring-do. The twelfth century was littered with strolling troubadours who wandered the land singing romantic songs about the heroes of the day, and one such song was sung about Fulk II Fitz Warine. The custom in those days was to send the sons of noblemen for training at a neighbouring castle, where they were taught knightly skills and virtues. Young Fulk was packed off to Ludlow Castle, where the lord was Sir Josce de Dynan. Sir Josce had two daughters, Sybille and Hawyse. Hawyse de Dynan was of a similar age to Fulk, who apparently was forlorn at being away from his family, his sad face earning him the nickname Fulk le Brun.

Fulk soon found himself embroiled in a bitter dispute between Sir Josce and his neighbour Sir Gilbert de Lacy, who claimed title to Ludlow Castle through a familial link. (The building of Ludlow Castle had been started by Roger de Lacy.) By Fulk's 18th birthday the dispute had escalated into open conflict. One summer's day Ludlow Castle was attacked by de Lacy and his forces, and when the assault was repelled and de Lacy was forced to retreat, Sir Josce gave chase, catching up with his enemy on the road to Bromfield. Unfortunately de Lacy's men rallied and in the ensuing fight Sir Josce found himself in mortal peril.

Fulk II saw this from the castle ramparts and decided to take action. Armed with only a Danish war axe, and mounted on the first horse he saw (a pack-horse), Fulk spurred to the rescue. Although still a novice in the art of battle, Fulk cleaved two of de Lacy's men, and forced the wounded Sir Arnald de Lys to yield; seeing this, Sir Gilbert also surrendered. The two lords were taken back to Ludlow Castle as prisoners and housed in Penover Tower.

For his bravery, a grateful Sir Josce rewarded Fulk with the hand of his daughter, the beautiful Hawyse. The happy couple were married by the bishop of Hereford, and the union was blessed with a son, who they named Fulk III Fitz Warine.

Ludlow Castle.

Meanwhile, the chivalrous Sir Josce treated his two prisoners well, allowing them visits from his wife and daughters, and other servants of the house, including Marion de la Bruere, Lady de Dynan's chief serving woman. Marion fell head over heels in love with the handsome Sir Arnald, who promised to marry her if she would help him to escape, which she did.

One day when Sir Josce was away from the castle, Marion, feigning illness, sent a message to Sir Arnald, reminding him of his promise. He replied, telling her he would come to take her away, and that she should let down a rope from the tower.

Sir Arnald arrived at the appointed time and scaled the tower, and while he and Marion were in bed making love, a body of soldiers followed him up the rope, killed the defenders, and hoisted the de Lacy banner.

When she realised that Sir Arnald had betrayed her, Marion snatched up his sword and stabbed him to death, before killing herself by leaping from a high window in the tower.

On dark nights when spirits roam the earth, the ghostly figure of the beautiful Marion de la Bruere appears to haunt the castle ruins. Some say that occasionally the ghost of Sir Arnald can also been seen.

~ *The Real Robin Hood* ~

When King Henry II came to the throne in 1154, things continued to go well for the Fitz Warines. In 1160, Fulk Fitz Warine senior (Fulk II) was given the prestigious task of arming and provisioning Dover Castle, confirming that the king held the Fitz Warines in high esteem.

Like his father before him, young Fulk junior (Fulk III) was packed off to court to learn his knightly duties, where he was raised with the king's sons, chiefly the youngest, Prince John, as they were of a similar age. Prince John has always been portrayed as a moody and mean fellow, and the story goes that the he fell out with Fulk – big time.

One day when the two lads were alone playing a game of chess, Prince John, who was probably losing, snatched up the chessboard and smashed it over Fulk's head. Fulk retaliated with a kick to John's chest that sent the young prince flying backwards, banging his head on a wall and knocking him senseless. John complained bitterly to his father, the king, who apparently chastised his son for being ever argumentative, and because he probably deserved what he got, then had his tutor thrash him. From that day on, John hated Fulk.

In 1164, the king granted the Lordship of Whittington Castle to Geoffrey de Vere, and then the following year to prominent Welsh leader Roger de Powys; Whittington had become part of Wales in 1140.

Things changed again when King Henry died and Richard I succeeded to the throne. The Lionheart treated young Fulk and his brothers – Philip the Red, William, John, and Alan – as favourites, definitely irking Prince John. Together

Whittington Castle.

with their cousin Baldwin of Hodnet, the five Warine brothers are recorded as being knights of strength, goodness and courage. When Richard I left England on his crusade, Fulk senior (Fulk II) was appointed Warden of the Marches. He died in 1197 or 1198.

However, things took a turn for the worse when in 1199 Richard died suddenly, and John was crowned king. Fulk III was summoned to Castle Baldwin (Montgomery Castle) by King John to discuss the Marches, only to be met by Sir Morys Fitz Roger de Powis. Fulk was advised that Sir Morys was now Warden of the Marches, and a member of the king's council. Sir Morys also entreated the king to reconfirm his right to Whittington Castle and its lands, as had his father, and King John agreed to this.

In retaliation, Fulk withdrew his homage to King John; subsequently Sir Morys called Fulk a liar, and was struck in the face by Fulk's brother, William. The Warine brothers and their cohorts rode away condemned as outlaws. King John sent a body of fifteen knights after them, but these strong knights were forced to withdraw. Fulk and his companions took the advice of his mother at Alderbury and fled the country.

Later, Fulk returned to England, only to discover that during his self-imposed exile his mother had died. Determined to win back his rightful inheritance, Fulk and his cohorts travelled to Babbing Forest near Whittington, but unfortunately they were seen and once again were pursued. In the ensuing one-sided skirmish, both Fulk and Sir Morys sustained wounds. Still, Fulk and his men managed to escape, evading capture on many occasions and wreaking havoc by robbing the king's representatives and tax inspectors. Fulk even found time to marry the beautiful heiress Maud le Vavasour, widow of the powerful Lancastrian baron Theobald Walter. Maud was a wealthy woman, and it is said that King John wanted to marry her himself, thus further inflaming the feud between the two men.

The outlaws learned that Sir Morys was planning to journey to Shrewsbury and set an ambush near Nesscliff. He succeeded in this and Sir Morys, fifteen of his knights, and the four sons of Guy Fitz Candelou were slain. King John raised an army intent on defeating Fulk.

Welsh prince Llewelyn ap Iowerth, who was married to King John's sister, Joan, joined forces with Fulk and the two armies clashed at Ffordd Gam Elen, neither gaining the advantage. Fulk, now back at Whittington, subsequently attacked the king's castle at Ruyton, held by John le Strange, who together with Sir Henry de Audley of Weston-under-Redcastle was commanded by the king to raise an army to retake Whittington Castle. Fulk ambushed them at the Pass of Myddle, then retreated to Whittington.

King John's solution to this stalemate was to offer Llewelyn peace in return for the betrayal of Fulk Fitz Warine. Taking no chances, Fulk and his companions once again sought refuge in France.

On Fulk's return from France, King John finally decided he had had enough and pardoned Fulk, together with fifty-two of his followers, including his brothers William, Philip, and John; Baldwin of Hodnet and his brother Stephen; Roger, John, and Richard de Preston; Henry de Pontesbury; Philip de Hanwood; and Philip de Wem. Fulk was permitted to retain Whittington and its estates.

Maud died in 1226 and was laid to rest in Fulk's foundation Alberbury Priory.

Fulk III married a second time, to Clarice de Auberville. He lived another forty years until his death in 1258, aged 86.

WILDERLEY

~ You Put a Spell on Me ~

Not far from Pulverbach is the village of Wilderley where there lived an old woman named Betty Chidley, who often begged for food at the farmhouse of Mr and Mrs Ambler. One day Mrs Ambler was heating up a mixture of meal and milk with which to feed the young calves, as she did every day, when old Betty wandered in. She saw the mixture and begged to be given a bowl of it. Mrs Ambler, no doubt fed up with the old woman's constant intrusion, flatly refused to give her any. Old Betty responded mysteriously by predicting that the calves would not eat the 'supping' now, then wandered off. Mrs Ambler, though puzzled by the old woman's words, thought no more of it, and took the mixture to the cowshed. However, the young calves refused to touch it; three times she tried with no success. Mrs Ambler recalled old Betty Chidley's prediction, and was convinced the old woman had laid some sort of a curse. She sent for Betty, who refused to return to the farm; however, she did agree to advise a few choice words for the farmer's wife to say. Mrs Ambler chanted, 'My God, bless the calves,' but it had no affect for still the calves refused to eat. Again Mrs Ambler begged old Betty to break the spell; and finally with a piercing glance that asked the question 'Who's begging now?', she agreed, simply omitting the word 'my'. 'God bless the calves' chanted the old woman, and immediately the calves, began to eat.

WILLEY

~ *The Whipper-In* ~

This is the curious eighteenth-century tale of the whipper-in at Willey Hall, near Broseley (a whipper-in is a huntsman's assistant who drives straying hounds back into the pack). His name was Tom Moody of the Broseley Hunt, and he told everyone that would listen that his worst fear was being buried alive.

The story goes that he reputedly implored his employer, Lord Forester, to do everything in his power to ensure that he was definitely dead before being interred, requesting that his lordship follow his list of specific instructions, which were as follows: that he be buried under the Yew trees in the churchyard at Barrow; that a specific method of delivery to the graveyard was followed, with his whip, boots, cap and spurs being hung from either side of the saddle of his horse, plus the brush tail of the last fox chased and killed; that a couple of foxhounds would act as mourners; that after his coffin had been lowered into the grave, three loud halloos be given; and if at that point he didn't raise his head, then those present could safely conclude that he was well and truly dead.

When Tom died, his burial took place on 19 November 1796 and his list of conditions were followed to the letter. However, Tom Moody's ghost, complete with ghostly hound at his side, is still said to haunt the place, reappearing ready to join with the hunt.

Tom Moody's grave, St Giles' churchyard, Barrow, near Broseley.

WISTANSTOWE

~ *Dirty Deeds* ~

Wistanstowe has been a settlement since Roman times. It is a place where Anglo Saxon myths and legends, central to the cult of St Wigstan (otherwise known as St Wystan), abound.

Wigstan was the son of Wigmond, King of Mercia around 840 AD. Upon the death of his father, Wigstan may have reigned briefly before being killed by his successor, Beorhtwulf, who is said to have been his Godfather. The ambitious Beorhtwulf had hatched a devious plan to marry his son, Beorhfrith, to Wigstan's widowed mother. Wigstan objected to the marriage, and Beorhtwulf's response was to have him killed.

The site of his martyrdom has been claimed to be Wistanstowe. A cult relating to Wigstan's martyrdom developed soon after his death.

WOODCOTE

~ *The Monkey Man* ~

This is the tale about a strange event that took place late on 21 January 1879. A carter had been hired to deliver the luggage of a party of guests from a large house in Ranton in Staffordshire to Woodcote Hall, near Newport in Shropshire.

On their return journey the driver and his horse were tired as they clip-clopped along the road, which was lit only by a waning moon. When they reached the place where the road passes over the Shropshire Canal at around 10 p.m., a large black creature with huge white eyes sprang out of the bushes at the side of the road and leapt onto the horse's back. The startled driver grabbed his whip and

Woodcote Hall, near Newport.

attempted to force the simian creature off the horse, but when the whip passed through the creature's body as if wasn't there, the driver's terror turned to blind panic. He dropped the whip as the screaming horse, with the ghostly creature still on its back, broke into a canter. The driver closed his eyes during the headlong rush, opening them only when the bridge had been crossed. The horse halted and the driver saw that the creature had disappeared. Once his heart rate had returned to normal, the driver urged his reluctant horse on as fast as his tiredness would allow, soon reaching the Staffordshire village of Woodseaves, a mile or so from the bridge.

In a hostelry the driver told his terrifying tale to a group of men who were still enjoying a drink, scaring one of the drinkers so much that the man, who lived on the other side of the bridge, was too frightened to go home, and stayed in the village with one of his friends. Eventually the cart driver's courage returned sufficiently for him to continue his journey home, although in truth the man was still in a state of shock. When home was reached the driver took to his bed still in a state of fright and stayed there for several days. The day after the incident the driver's whip was searched for and found at the spot where the driver said it had been dropped.

Now comes the even more curious part. The story became the talk of the area, embellished by others, who added all manner of variations. A few days later the employer of the driver received a visit from the police, who asked for details of the robbery at the bridge on the night of 21 January, to which the employer replied that there had been no robbery. He told the story as his driver had related it to him. The policeman shrugged and said he knew what it was: the monkey man. He explained that the creature is a ghost that appears at the bridge every so often, ever since a man fell into the canal and was drowned.

So beware those who travel across High Bridge No. 39 of the Shropshire Union Canal, known as the Grub Street Cutting, for the monkey man might get you!

WOOLSTON

~ Another Well, Well ~

In Woolston there is yet another of Shropshire's numerous holy wells. This one is dedicated to St Winifred.

The water, which runs sparkling and clear into two stone basins set in an alcove, is said to hold the power to heal all manner of wounds. Not only that but it can make bruises disappear (in time of course), and can also mend broken bones. Apparently there was once a local man who told the story of his broken arm being healed after treating it with holy water from this well. He explained that his daily routine involved early morning visits to the well, where he would dip his arm into

St Winifred's Well, Woolston.

The Abbey church of St Peter and St Paul, Shrewsbury.

the water, and, hey presto, the broken bone healed. He never said how long it took, but did reveal that his doctor had told him to do this.

St Winifred's Well is covered over by a half-timbered construction shaped like a cruciform, with a chapel-like roof. Part of the structure contains work from the fourteenth century and earlier. It is said to have been constructed on the orders of Queen Margaret, wife of King Henry VI, to commemorate the spot where, many years earlier, St Winifred's remains had been laid down during transit from Holywell to Shrewsbury Abbey by the monks that had been sent out to bring the saint to the town. Legend has it that when the monks lifted the saint's remains, after enjoying their hard-earned rest, a spring immediately burst out of the earth from the very spot where the body had lain.

St Winifred was a seventh-century Welsh martyr. Her remains were obtained by Prior Robert Pennant, who had been dispatched to Wales to find a suitable religious relic for Shrewsbury Abbey by the Abbot to draw in the paying pilgrims. Pennant returned in 1138 with the bones of St Gwenfrewi (St Winifred). And thus, the relics enshrined, the Abbey became a major centre of pilgrimage.

WREKIN

~ *The Needle's Eye* ~

On the steepest face of the Shropshire hill called the Wrekin is a curious opening in the rock known as the Needle's Eye. Local legend claims it appeared at the time of the Crucifixion when the rocks were formed. Towards the bottom of the fissure, the hole widens sufficiently to allow a person to pass through. There are two legends surrounding the Needle's Eye.

The first concerns any young lady making her first visit to the Wrekin. If she scrambles through the hole, she must be accompanied by a male friend who in turn must stand on the other side of the hole ready to greet her with a kiss. However, if she refuses to be kissed, he can claim a forfeit of a ribbon, or a handkerchief, or any piece of coloured material that she may be wearing.

The second legend states that any young lady who slips through the hole and turns to look back, will never be married. The exact origin or purpose of this belief has, like many other such superstitions, been lost in the mists of time.

X

XANTHIPPE

Few counties have towns or villages whose name begins with the letter X, and Shropshire is no exception to this, therefore, with the reader's indulgence, the author has included the following piece of curious information.

The dictionary definition tells us that a Xanthippe is the formal name for a shrewish woman, or a scold – one who gossips maliciously. The word itself is taken from the Greek name of the wife of the famous philosopher Socrates (not the famous one-time captain of the Brazilian World Cup football team). Greek writer Xenophon, in his *Symposium* written in the late 360s BC, describes a kind of themed dinner party with discussion and entertainment that had supposedly taken place around 422 BC. The get-together was attended by Socrates and a few companions, the themes being: love, wisdom, virtue, laughter, beauty and desire. Xenophon describes Socrates' wife as having 'an undesirable temperament, and the hardest to get along with of all women there are.' In contrast to Xenophon's view, the great Plato described Xanthippe as a devoted wife and mother. But whatever the lady's attributes or deficiencies, she somehow got stuck with Xenophon's description.

In this country in olden times, shrewish women were treated to a spell in a brank, otherwise known as a Scold's Bridle. This was a device made of metal strips formed into a head-sized cage or cowl, which had a metal spit that protruded into the victim's mouth where it depressed the tongue, thus preventing them from gossiping or being verbally horrid to fellow citizens. Sometimes the Xanthippe was sentenced to punishment on the ducking or cucking stool, which from medieval times was accepted as the main instrument used for inflicting pain and torture on criminals. Another description of a person sentenced to the ducking stool was a troublesome and angry type of woman, who by their constant brawling and wrangling of her neighbours, breaks the public peace and increases local discord, becoming a public nuisance to the neighbourhood; the ducking stool was supposed to 'cool her immoderate heat and to curb her tongue.'

As well as scolds, gossips, and shrewish or bad-tempered women, the ducking stool was also used to punish the crimes of prostitution, heresy and witchcraft.

Ducking was seen as a foolproof way of establishing whether or not the person accused was a witch. The accused was strapped or tied to the stool (a chair attached to a long beam), head and feet bare, wearing a shift, and ducked as mentioned earlier in this book. For the non-witches, the length of immersion varied; it sometimes lasted only a few seconds, for three or four dunks, but in some cases the immersions might be repeated continuously over the course of one day – it largely depended on the sharpness of the victim's tongue; there were no set rules to decide the harshness of the treatment.

An English poet by the name of Vincent Bourne, who lived between 1645 and 1747, composed a Latin poem about the ducking stool, which went: 'Astride it set but a Xanthippe, then twice or thrice virago dip ye ... Then say if ever Socratic school such lesson taught as ducking-stool.'

Eighteenth- and nineteenth-century reformers called for more humane punishments and so the practice of dunking died out.

Y

YOCKLETON

~ Goblins? ~

A very odd happening took place at Yockleton Park before 1783. Farmer Nicholls and his large family lived there quite happily. One summer a man described as a 'Welshman' approached the farmer for work, and was duly hired to help gather in the harvest. The man proved to be a good worker and so when he asked to be allowed to stay on through the winter, the farmer had no hesitation in saying yes.

Just after midnight on one freezing night during the Christmas festival, known in Shropshire as the 'Mystic Twelve Days' (known long before the advent of Christianity as the witching time, when spirits are abroad), the entire family were roused from their slumber by a terrible noise coming from downstairs. They described the noise as being like heavy furniture being dragged around the room, accompanied by loud clanking and rumbling. The farmer roused the other farmhands in the house and all trooped nervously down the stairs, and to their amazement found – nothing!

All the chairs and table were where they should be, nothing was out of place and other than themselves, no one was to be seen or heard; all was quiet and as it should be.

The Welshman offered to go outside into the blackness of the night to investigate the mystery further, but the farmer, being unnerved by the whole experience, refused to allow the door to be opened. But the Welshman insisted, and despite being sceptical the farmer agreed, providing that he and he alone went outside. The farmhouse door was opened sufficiently wide enough to allow only the Welshman to pass through and was then rapidly closed and barred.

Inside, the family and farmhands listened and waited, but the Welshman never returned. What became of him no one ever knew. His wages remained at the farm – unclaimed.

Legends ask the question: was the Welshman a real living and breathing person or was he a trusty 'drudging goblin'? A drudging goblin takes service with an earthly master, and one day without warning vanishes mysteriously. There are parallels for this legend in Northern mythology.

Z

ZEPPELINS

~ The Great Zeppelin Raid ~

During the First World War on the night of 31 January 1916, a German Zeppelin was seen in the skies over Shropshire. Great Western Railway records state that their staff first sighted the Zeppelin in the skies near Banbury, Oxfordshire. The airship carried on to Birmingham and then to Shrewsbury, reaching the town at around 10.10. p.m. It was later spotted over Welshpool, Craven Arms and Bridgnorth.

A force of nine German airships led by the L21 and the L13 Zeppelins left their bases at Friedrichshafen and Lowenthal on 31 January 1916, crossing the Norfolk coast at around 5.50 p.m., their target being Liverpool and its docks. As darkness grew, navigation, which was made by measuring airspeed against time plus observation whenever possible, became increasingly difficult, hindered also by mist and fog. The L21, commanded by Kapitan-Leutnant Max Dietrich, increased its speed, and saw lights below which Dietrich took to be Manchester, but which was actually Derby. Dietrich turned west expecting to reach Liverpool, but below all he saw was blackness. Thinking he had overshot the target and that he was flying over the Irish Sea, he turned south-east. However, he was now flying over Shropshire. When he finally saw lights below, it was not Birkenhead, but the Black Country. His bombs fell on Tipton, Bradley and Wednesbury, and then on Walsall, wreaking havoc, and leaving a scene of death and destruction in their wake. Another of the airships, the L19, under the command of Kapitan-Leutnant Loewe, seeing the fires raging below, dropped his bombs on Wednesbury, before heading towards the east coast. The L19 came down in the North Sea after engine trouble and taking heavy rifle-fire from the Dutch coast.

This raid gave the Midlands a tragic taste of aerial warfare. Initial casualty figures were published as being 61 dead and 101 injured. No bombs fell on Shropshire.

Named after their inventor, Count Ferdinand von Zeppelin, a retired German Army officer who flew his first Zeppelin in 1900, the Zeppelins were a fabric-covered rigid metal framework containing a number of individual gasbags, filled with hydrogen. The Germans called a halt to Zeppelin raids in 1917, by which time 77 of the 115 German airships had been shot down or totally disabled.

Postscipt

Well, that's it folks. I've loved writing it – I hope you enjoyed reading it.